M000188757

Til mamma og pappa

The Feminine and Nihilism:

Luce Irigaray with Nietzsche and Heidegger

Ellen Mortensen

The Feminine and Nihilism:

Luce Irigaray with Nietzsche and Heidegger

SCANDINAVIAN UNIVERSITY PRESS
Oslo - Copenhagen - Stockholm

Scandinavian University Press (Universitetsforlaget AS),
P.O. Box 2959 Tøyen, N-0608 Oslo, Norway
Fax +47 22 57 53 53

Stockholm office
SCUP, Scandinavian University Press
P.O. Box 3255, S-103 65 Stockholm, Sweden
Fax +46 8 20 99 82

Copenhagen office
Scandinavian University Press AS
P.O. Box 54, DK-1002 København K, Denmark
Fax +45 33 32 05 70

© Scandinavian University Press (Universitetsforlaget AS) 1994

ISBN 82-00-21674-8

Published with a grant from the Norwegian Research Council

All rights reserved. No part of this publication may be reproduced,
stored in a retrieval system, or transmitted, in any form or by any
means, without the prior permission in writing of Scandinavian
University Press. Enquiries concerning reproduction outside these
terms and in other countries should be sent to the Rights Department,
Scandinavian University Press, Oslo, at the address above

Printed in Norway by A/S Foto-Trykk, Trøgstad 1994

Table of Contents

Acknowledgements

The publication of this book has been made possible in part due to a grant awarded by the Norwegian Research Council for Science and the Humanities.

I would like to thank Professor Próspero Saíz, Department of Comparative Literature, University of Wisconsin-Madison, for providing an intellectual climate in which my work has thrived. His astute criticism as well as his continuous support and friendship have been invaluable in this laborious process. I would also like to express my sincere gratitude to Professor Elaine Marks, Department of French, University of Wisconsin-Madison, who first introduced me to Irigaray's work and who has been a true intellectual as well as personal inspiration. I am also indebted to Professor Toril Moi, Department of Romance Languages, Duke University, and Professor Margaret Whitford, French Department, Queen Mary and Westfield College, University of London, both of whom have read earlier versions of the book and whose comments have been most helpful in reworking the manuscript.

In addition, I want to salute my colleagues, friends and family, both in the U.S. and in Norway, whose love and encouragement have helped me through the trials of this project. In this regard, I especially want to extend my thanks to Babette Wainwright, Mary Jo Bona, Sandra Adell, Paal Bjørby, Birger Angvik, Hans-Erik Aarset, Anka Ryall and Roy-Tommy Eriksen.

Bergen, June 1994

Ellen Mortensen

Introduction

When Luce Irigaray pronounces that sexual difference constitutes the most pressing question which remains to be thought in our epoch, she bases her argument on Martin Heidegger's insight that "each age is preoccupied with one thing, and one alone".[1] If we consent to this statement, then we must pay heed to how the question is posited. In order for a question to be posited, Martin Heidegger[2] argues, the answer has to be to pre-understood. Irigaray envisages that, for the question of sexual difference to be thought, a new fertility of thought, in her words, a new poetics,[3] would have to emerge. She claims that all previous attempts by philosophy, by science or by religion to raise the question of sexual difference have only occulted the problematic. However, in order

> [f]or the work of sexual difference to take place, a revolution in thought and ethics is needed. We must re-interpret the whole relationship between the subject and discourse, the subject and the world, the subject and the cosmic, the microcosmic and the macrocosmic.[4]

One of Irigraray's most famous pronouncements from *Speculum of the Other Woman*[5] reads as follows: "Every theory of the subject is always already appropriated by the masculine." By this she suggests that the feminine remains repressed, silenced, invisible and unheard within the phallogocentric discourses of philosophy, religion and science. The task of thinking lies therefore in the re-interpretation of what she nominates the technological machine of man-made languages. Thus, there is in her thinking a strong belief in the interconnectedness between the current global state of affairs and the dominant mode of thinking in the West. Some of the ecological, political and economic problems of our planet can in part be explained by this Western mode of thinking, which she sees as molded upon a morphology of the masculine sexual libidinal economy.

In the West, says Irigaray, there is a predominance of a masculine "hom(m)osexual" economy, which she defines as an exclusively masculine culture founded on a genealogy of the father and the son.[6] There exists a religious, legal, cultural, spiritual and libidinal bonding which symbolically unites men and which systematically excludes women or any manifestations of a symbolic of the feminine. The only function prescribed for women is as reproductive objects of exchange within this economy. For Irigaray, the masculine subject comes to represent all that is valued as positive within the binary system of meaning in Western thinking: conscious, rational, unified, solid, visible, eternal, spiritual, lofty, monolithic, etc. Conversely, the feminine (non-subject) figures as his negative Other, above and against which the masculine subject finds form and expression. Thus, within the signifying structures of the West, there exists no sexual difference of the subject. There is but one, the self-same, the masculine.

But if there is but one subject, it becomes necessary to inquire into what Irigaray coins the Other, otherwise nominated as the feminine, or *le féminin*. Irigaray speaks of the feminine as a nothing that resists representation. Nevertheless, *le féminin* finds a variety of expressions throughout her work. She refers to it as that which is repressed, fluid, mucous, near, tactile, material, elemental, aerial, marine, dark, silent, multiple, temporal, earthly, divine, nurturing, creative, ethical, etc. But it is necessary to investigate whether or not this (multiple) positing of *le féminin* remains locked within the comfortable boundaries of the metaphysics that she claims to subvert.

The eclectic threads of discourses at work in Irigaray's writings are all intertwined into Western philosophical discourses ranging from the Pre-Socratics, Plato, Aristotle, Descartes, Kant, Hegel, Nietzsche, Heidegger, Lévinas to Derrida. In addition, she inserts herself into a variety of other and implicated theoretical paradigms such as Freudian and Lacanian psychoanalysis, linguistics, Marxist political/economic theory, structuralist anthropology, French feminisms, Anglo-American feminisms, and other contemporary political and legal discourses.

Irigaray emphasizes the crucial role played by the Greeks for the destiny of Western thought. Greek literature and mythology form a core of resonance in her writing. Like Martin Heidegger, she believes that the coming of a new age of thinking necessitates a re-turn to the questions raised by the Pre-Socratics, and in ancient mythology. Irigaray insists that this enormously rich Pre-Hellenic epoch still hides enigmas that remain pressing for us to think about. Furthermore, in her search for a new ethic of the feminine, which she posits as key to the creation of a new thinking, Irigaray insists on the necessity of scrutinizing the religious discourses we have inherited. This implies an invention of new, as well as a resurrection of ancient, female deities. Contrary to masculine deities, these female deities will honor the feminine symbolic and will, she hopes, effect the end of sexual *in-difference* in religion and mythology as well as in language.

In Irigaray's hermeneutic of sexual difference, much emphasis is placed on the task of interpretation, or more specifically, re-interpretation. In her prophetic statements about the implications of the work of sexual difference, Irigaray claims that *all* is to be reinterpreted. However, the question of the Being of interpretation *per se* will have to be addressed. Thus, we will have to inquire whether or not the revolutionary work of this new thinking presumably finds its ground in interpretation or if, on the other hand, Irigaray seeks an-other foundation for her thinking.

This pivotal question of what constitutes the Being of interpretation needs to be addressed in order to determine the path of questioning that will follow.[7] Irigaray's strategy of re-interpretation raises the question of the status of the speaking/writing subject. In her retracing of Western metaphysics, be it in the form of a rereading of among others, Plato, Freud, Hegel, Descartes and Kant in *Speculum of the Other Woman*, or, of Lacan and Sade in *This Sex Which Is Not One*,[8] Irigaray attempts to subvert the comfortable position attributed to the masculine subject in an effort to open up a space for *sexual difference within the subject*. However, it is important to ask how Irigaray understands the ground or the Being of the subject and the implications this might have for her project of (re)interpretation.

While reluctantly ascribing to the (Lacanian) psychoanalytic view in regard to the construction of the subject, Irigaray laments the fact that the feminine does not have an imaginary of its own upon which the female subject might construct its "mirror image".[9] This *imago* later serves as a foundation for the construction of the sexed subject. The absence of such an *imago* is, in her opinion, one of the reasons why there is but one subject, namely the masculine. Irigaray asks what happens if we open up the question of an (absent) feminine subject for thought. Will this inquiry necessitate a *different* language, she asks. Implicit in her questioning is a proposed strategy for discursive action that would eventually undermine the sedimented language of metaphysics. In the following, she sketches out what such a strategy might entail:

> Then ... Turn everything upside down, inside out, back to front. *Rack it with radical convulsions*, carry back, reimport, those cries that her "body" suffers in her impotence to say what disturbs her. Insist also and deliberately upon those *blanks* in discourse which recall the places of her exclusion and which, by their *silent plasticity*, ensure the cohesion, the articulation, the coherent expansion of established forms.[10]

In this projected "radical convulsion" of language, Irigaray sketches out the contours of a deconstructive strategy. However, while she denounces phal-logo-centric language, she envisions a strategy which exceeds the mimetic. Her proposed intervention rests partly on the (female) subject's intentional subversion of these functions and structures. But her intervention relies primarily on the workings of unconscious effects. By effecting a release of some of the repressed (feminine) carnal excesses into language, Irigaray predicts that woman's unconscious will cause the walls of the phallic logic to crumble.

She furthermore denounces the present state of affairs in theory (under which she subsumes philosophy) and seems to distance herself from all of the dominant discursive practices.[11] Her diagnosis of the malaise of contemporary philosophy ironically and indirectly points both to Derridean deconstruction and Heideggerian ontology. Irigaray emphasizes the need to find other foundations and other works which will bring about a *different* logic from that of the first philosophy which has hitherto governed our horizon.

This book does not intend to cover all of Irigaray's work. It is primarily a close reading of her poetico-philosophic work, *Marine Lover of Friedrich Nietzsche*.[12] Through a lover's discourse on/with Nietzsche, Irigaray mimics and parodies the aphoristic *grand style* of the late(st) philosopher. Implicit in her inquiry into Nietzsche's texts is her search for the feminine, which she, like Derrida, understands within the question of *écriture*, as the possibility of an-other gaze, an-other speech and an-other language than those which have hitherto governed Western metaphysical thinking.

By strategically inserting herself in the openings of Nietzsche's writings and by listening to the silent *mater-ial* ground upon which he erects his philosophy, Irigaray retrieves that which has been muted in his discourse. This silence then serves as a potentiality for her exploration of sexual difference, or, for what she refers to as *le féminin*.

My reading will venture to deconstruct Irigaray's deconstructive reading of Nietzsche. In this double deconstructive gesture, I hope to make resonant some of the multiple *inter-texts*[13] that are put into play in her discourse, particularly Plato, Nietzsche and Heidegger. Attempts will be made to implicate Irigaray's questioning into the nihilism problematic as it is thought, primarily, by Nietzsche, and subsequently by Heidegger.

In *Marine Lover* Irigaray confronts the basic constituents of Nietzsche's thinking. As such it can be read as a meditation on Nietzsche's philosophy of will to power – a philosophy which for her may prove to be partially fruitful in providing her with new paths of thinking in the quest for sexual difference.[14] However, by unveiling Nietzsche's apparent complicity in Western metaphysics, Irigaray's deconstruction of his oeuvre also warns against premature and facile appropriations of Nietzsche in the name of any "-ism".

But when Irigarary sets out to think through Nietzsche's philosophy of will to power in all its complexity, the question of (sexual) *difference* is inserted at the heart of her inquiry. How does/does not Nietzsche think (sexual) difference, Irigaray asks. And if he does, – how does (sexual) difference figure within his philosophy?

I will argue that it is illuminating to read Irigaray's meditation on Nietzsche in light of the nihilism problematic. Nietzsche defines nihilism as the historical movement whereby "all values hitherto have been devalued".[15] This means that man has lost the ground upon which his moral and reason-able universe had been erected. No longer can he be assured of the existence of universal truth or absolute value. Nietzsche provides an answer to this unfortunate state of affairs through his conception of will to power, wherein man finds the imperative to shape his own existence and his universe through an act of transvaluation.[16] This transvaluation, which revalues all previous values, has no universal validity. However, Nietzsche's transvaluing subject has gained the power to define his own being as value, without being restrained by any universal (moral/epistemological) law. Man wilfully inscribes the circumference of his own being through his perspectival perception of what **is**.

It will be important to uncover whether she, in her reading of Nietzsche, identifies the sexed subject as a problem related to propositional thinking, or, whether she, instead, approaches it as an ontological question. For Irigaray, the subject's Being is ultimately grounded in the materiality of the body which provides the matrix for the construction of every subject. We will have to ask whether or not this implies an evasion of the question of an ontological ground and whether she operates within the derivative framework of an already existing metaphysical Platonic division between the material and the spiritual.

Or, does Irigaray's thinking on this primary *locus* of the (M)Other in any way reside in the proximity of Heidegger's thinking on the question of the ontological difference between Being and beings? "Language is the house of Being in which man exists by dwelling, in that he belongs to the truth of Being, guarding it," Martin Heidegger writes in his "Letter on Humanism".[17] Irigaray refers to this quote by Heidegger and the link between the subject and language when she makes an insightful observation on the relationship between Lacan and Heidegger:

> It is probably from this conception of the relationship between the subject and language that Lacan has taken his definition of the unconscious. The expression "The unconscious is structured like a language" is quite close to that put forth by Martin Heidegger: "Man acts as though he were the shaper and master of language, while in fact language remains the master of man." (cf. "Poetically Man Dwells" in *Poetry, Language, Thought*, trans. by Albert Hofstadter (New York: Harper & Row, 1971, p. 215)[18].

Another question to be pursued in relation to Irigaray's work, is that of the Being of language in her texts. For example, what is the pre-understanding that informs the following statement concerning language:

> Language, no matter how formal it is, has nourished itself by blood, by flesh, by elemental matter(s). By whom and by what has it nourished itself? How to repay this debt? Are we forced to produce increasingly formal mechanisms, techniques, which turn against man? Is such an inverted result caused by this mother who has given him a living body? And which he fears accordingly as the unpaid (debt) between her and him.[19]

In another passage from the same work, Irigaray invokes (in a parenthesis) Heidegger's Heraklitus-seminar[20] in which he states that Western metaphysics has not even begun to say what there might *be* to the body. Irigaray argues that the body constitutes this first "house" which man receives and which determines the possibility of his coming to the world and the possible opening of a horizon of thought, of poetry, and of celebration with the god(s). Heidegger's contribution reveals the difficulties involved in any appropriative reading of texts. It also serves to alert attention to the problematic of language as it intrudes upon any theoretical interrogation. As such, his work has laid the foundation and paved the way for both Lacanian psychoanalysis and Derridean deconstruction.

By reflecting on Heidegger's thinking on the relationship of Dasein to its Being-in-the-world with Others,[21] Jacques Lacan developed his understanding of the speaking subject's relation to the symbolic order which is again in thrall to the Phallus/Other. Lacan carefully studied Heidegger's thinking on the *logos*[22] before working out what has been nominated his early *Dasein* psychoanalysis. As the above quote indicates, Irigaray clearly makes the explicit connection between Heidegger's thinking and that of Lacan when it comes to the question of language.

It should be noted that Irigaray is herself a trained linguist,[23] and that a substantial part of her work deals with the problem of language, be it as part of her broader philosophical concern in reading the philosophical tradition, be it in her contributions to the psychoanalytic debate through her controversial readings of Freud and Lacan, or be it in her specific work in linguistics.

It is my conviction that Heidegger's work constitutes the veiled sub-text which informs not only Irigaray's reading of Nietzsche, but also those readings of the two dominant father figures that are echoed in her work, namely Derrida and Lacan. And, perhaps most importantly, I believe that the Heidegger-Nietzsche nexus constitutes the most overlooked and silenced part of the appropriations of Irigaray's work. In my critical intervention, I hope to be able to dwell in the proximity of Heidegger's thinking and thereby carefully integrate some of his most pondered questions into my discussion.

CHAPTER I:
Reading Irigaray and the Question of Appropriation

As Nietzsche has become the battleground on which the philosophic *polemos* has taken place in the 20th century, so Irigaray has become the target for and a symptom of feminist[1] appropriations in the United States and in Britain, as well as on the European Continent. But for the most part, recent appropriations of Luce Irigaray have tended to enframe her writing into one dominant interpretative model, namely psychoanalysis.

One of the most prolific appropriators of Irigaray in the United States, Jane Gallop, has entitled her work The *Daughter's Seduction: Feminism and Psychoanalysis.*[2] In this work, she introduces Luce Irigaray playing the female lead, opposite Lacan. Gallop here performs an imaginative reading of *This Sex Which Is Not One*, in which Irigaray figures in the role of the (feminist) daughter of the father figures of psychoanalysis, Freud/Lacan.

Likewise, in her review of *Amante marine de Friedrich Nietzsche*, Elizabeth L. Berg exclusively emphasizes the psychoanalytic dimension of her work when she asserts that "[all] of Irigaray's work is in some sense to be understood as a dialogue with Lacan, although his name is spectacularly missing from her books".[3]

For the most part, the reception of Irigaray's work has been limited to the two texts that were first translated into English, namely *Speculum of the Other Woman* and *This Sex Which Is Not One*. Toril Moi's *Sexual/Textual Politics*[4] constitutes yet another comprehensive reading of Irigaray's work to date. However, even though she includes references to the entire body of Irigaray's writings, she relegates to the margins her treatment of Irigaray's philosophical works, and, like most of her predecessors, focuses instead on Irigaray's psychoanalytic work in *Speculum* and in *This Sex*.

Only a few scholars, like Margaret Whitford,[5] Elizabeth Grosz,[6] and Naomi Schor,[7] have attempted to tackle her complete work. Among these, the work of Margaret Whitford stands out in its rigorous treatment of Irigaray's text from a philosophical, as well as a psychoanalytic, perspective. Whitford argues in her assessment of Irigaray for "the psychoanalytic dimension of Iriga-ray's work to be taken seriously".[8] But in Whitford's groundbreaking work, *Luce Irigaray: Philosophy in the Feminine*, a lucid and engaging reading of Irigaray's whole corpus, Whitford also argues for the necessity to treat Irigaray as a philosophical thinker. In addition, with the publication of *The Irigaray Reader*, Whitford introduces the Anglo-American reader to a broad specter of Iriga-ray's texts. At the same time, Whitford provides an excellent intro-duction to the major tenets of Irigaray's thinking.

Elizabeth Grosz' reading of Irigaray provides yet another refreshing perspective in the reception of Irigaray. Like Whitford, Grosz emphasizes the philosophical nature of Irigaray's project, but attempts at the same time to discuss the political implications of her work.

In my view, Irigaray's writing can best be characterized as a philosophical intervention. That is not to say that psychoanalysis does not figure centrally within her body of work. True, as a trained and licenced psychoanalyst, Irigaray practises her trade (despite being expelled from Lacan's *école freudienne* upon her publication of *Speculum*).[9] And, in her writing, she certainly pur-sues an inquiry into (Lacanian/Freudian) psychoanalysis even as she ventures to deconstruct its discursive foundation.

However, there has been a certain blindness to the complexity of her work and the intricate inter-texts that constitute the fabric of her thinking. For me, Irigaray is aspiring to be a thinker, in the sense that she foresees "the end of metaphysics" and the "task of thinking"[10] that lie ahead. In order to do justice to this complex web of textuality, into which the major philosophemes of our Western metaphysical tradition are interwoven, careful attention must be given to her painstaking meditation on this tradition.

It is interesting to note that few critics have seriously attempted to address her readings of the Pre-Socratics, of Plato and Aristotle, of Descartes, of Kant and Hegel, of Nietzsche, of Heidegger, or of Lévinas. With the exception of Whitford, Grosz, and Schor, almost all interpretations have exclusively concentrated on her psychoanalytic work. Her philosophic work, which constitutes the better part of her production, has for the most part been silenced or ignored. I therefore contend that the majority of the appropriators of Irigaray have remained deaf to the profundity and breadth of her thinking, due to this selective focus. Through a simplistic enframing of her texts into an already limited scope, most readers of Irigaray fail to pay heed to some of her most thought-provoking questions.

Sometimes, these readings have instead produced a series of ideological debates,[11] most of which are critical of her contribution.[12] One of the most pervasive criticisms of Irigaray's work has centered around the question of essentialism. In her essay, "This Essentialism Which Is Not One", Naomi Schor convincingly exposes the confusion that reigns in relation to what essentialism supposedly bespeaks. She delineates four different forms of essentialism and reveals how each form trails with it a set of presuppositions and questions asked.[13] However, this debate has failed to raise the appropriate questions that could address Irigaray's philosophic concerns. Due in part to this inability to read her thinking on difference within the context of the dominant philosophemes in our tradition and due partly to the preoccupations of the theoretical and political/ideological agendas of the respective appropriators, much of Irigaray's work remains obscurely veiled for most Anglo-American readers.

Irigaray has also been criticized for her mimetic strategy in her deconstruction of Western metaphysical language. Toril Moi, among others, warns of the political dangers associated with Irigaray's mimetic strategy. In addition, she accuses Irigaray of attempting to define "woman"[14] in the process. But Irigaray never claims to be able to reflect *le féminin*. According to Irigaray, what woman or the maternal might be, cannot possibly be reflected in theoretical or philosophical language, since its edifice rests on the silencing of the primordial ground from which all beings emerge. Thus, when she mimes and mimics this metaphysical language, she does not adhere to the demarcations and the categories through which it operates. Rather, she attempts to listen to that "other" meaning which has been silenced, or which has escaped the mirror altogether.

This does not mean, however, that she claims to have created another language that is true to a feminine mimetic. Rather, she aligns herself with Lacan in his assertion that there is but one language, namely the one which speaks a phallic symbolic. How, and in what way woman as a subject enters into this symbolic and how she could possibly subvert its solidity, constitutes an important part of her work. However, in order to investigate this problem fully, the question of appropriation has to be broached.

Furthermore, what is approached in Irigaray's inquiry is the question of the Being of language. It is not merely a question of a subjective positionality guided by (a political) intentionality, which either attests to the good or the ill will of the subject. Rather, for Irigaray, what is at stake is the ontological possibility of *parler femme* in Western languages. And this question cannot be broached through or subsumed under any ideological or historiological concern.[15]

In my reading, Irigaray does not exclusively understand the problem of positionality in ideological terms. Rather, she raises the problem as an ontological foundational question concerning the Being of the speaking subject. And she knows full well that the philosophical discourse functions as a foundational discourse for all scientific and political discourses.[16] Her questions are: Can there be a feminine subject in Western languages? How could woman possibly emerge and be heard? By what strategy can we make this absence appear?

In "This Essentialism Which Is Not One", Naomi Schor responds to Moi's denunciation of Irigaray as an essentialist by adding a different emphasis:

My argument is contrario: that Irigaray's production of a positive theory of femininity is not an aberration, a sin to extend the theological metaphor, rather the logical extension of her deconstruction of the specular logic of saming. [...] For finally the question posed by Irigaray's attempts to theorize feminine specificity – which is not to be confused with "defining" woman, a task she writes is better left to men – is the question of difference *within* difference. Irigaray's wager is that difference can be reinvented.[17]

For Schor, when Irigaray invokes the term *mimesis*, it is as part of a strategy of miming, a masquerade to which women have traditionally been subjected, but which within this new affirmation might be reappropriated in order to pursue a radical new difference. Naomi Schor refers to the following passage in *This Sex* in which Irigaray delineates her strategy:

> There is, in an initial phase, perhaps only one "path", the one historically assigned to the feminine: that of *mimicry*. One must assume the feminine role deliberately. Which means already to convert a form of subordination into an affirmation, and thus to begin to thwart it. [...] To play with mimesis is thus, for a woman, to try to recover the place of her exploitation by discourse, without allowing herself to be simply reduced to it. It means to resubmit herself – inasmuch as she is on the other side of the "perceptible" of "matter" – to "ideas", in particular to ideas about herself, that are elaborated in/by a masculine logic, but so as to make "visible", by an effect of playful repetition, what was supposed to remain invisible: the cover-up of a possible operation of the feminine in language. It also means "to unveil" the fact that, if women are such good mimics, it is because they are not simply resorbed in this function. *They also remain elsewhere*: another case of the persistence of "matter", but also of "sexual pleasure".[18]

In her parodic stance against and within masculine discourse, Irigaray appropriates *mimesis*, not as a reflective device to mirror *le féminin*, but instead as a deconstructive strategy to break discursive integrity of this specular language by listening to the excesses of the sensible/material which it cannot reflect, but which resides "elsewhere".

Most importantly, Schor insists on another meaning of the polysemic word *mimesis* in Irigaray's work, namely that which connotes a Nietzschean notion of transvaluation. Read in this sense, the strategy of *mimesis* follows Nietzsche's thinking on the workings of nihilism in Western metaphysics, which attests to the devaluation of all values. However, through the act of transvaluation, which embraces the workings of nihilism by miming its effect, Nietzsche at the same time affirms a different value, whereby that which has been devalued becomes trans-valued. Zarathoustra, as the over-man, can in this context be seen as a transvaluation of the "human, all-too-human" man.

Similarly, femininity as it has been defined within this traditional metaphysical framework, which posits an opposition between the "sensuous" and the "supra-sensuous", has been devalued as inferior to masculinity. Femininity was attributed less value than masculinity since it was associated with the "sensuous" and "material", which is subject to change and de-formation by temporality. Masculinity, on the other hand, was valued through its supposed proximity to the "supra-sensuous" which remains solidly eternal and permanent in its "ideality". By miming femininity, and by embracing the nihilism that permeated these categories, Irigaray has produced its transvaluation: *le féminin*.

Schor's reinterpretation of Irigaray's use of mimeticism has provided a new avenue towards understanding Irigaray's writings in the light of a broader philosophical inquiry. As she also points out, Irigaray's quest is not for the essence of femininity, but rather an attempt to pursue a different understanding of mater-ialism that has not always already been predetermined by the Platonic schema of the dichotomy between the "sensuous" and the "supra-sensuous". In her projection of an elemental cosmology, Irigaray instead invokes the forgotten memory of the Pre-Socratics, whose ontological thinking on the elements becomes a point of departure for her thinking on *le féminin* in its materiality.

Irigaray's writings, along with those of Hélène Cixous and Julia Kristeva, have had a tremendous impact on the feminist inquiry in literature and theory during the last decade. Due to the widespread interest in their works, a new trend in literary/theoretical productions has taken place which has sought to detect "difference" in numerous (predominantly female) texts. What I find somewhat disquieting in regard to this activity, is a reduction of Irigaray's work into an applied methodology of reading.[19]

This particular form of appropriation treats her work as a tool for interpretation to be applied on other texts. The result is usually a difference in sameness, which for the most part claims to have discovered a feminine difference in texts which have hitherto been blind to sexual difference. The problem I detect in such a practice is that none of the appropriators deal with Irigaray's question of sexual difference, but focus instead on what they believe to be the answer, found in the texts that are being read.

What is lost in this form of appropriation is the complex meditation undertaken by Irigaray in relation to these questions. We are left with an army of (sometimes) well-intentioned readings, which make claims to have freed the feminine from its discursive confinements. But, what happens if we take seriously Irigaray's assumption that difference/*le féminin* is not present? What would happen to these benevolent readings that seek to identify difference if what Irigaray attempts to think is an *aletheic féminin*? Would not these readings crumble, when the foundations of their appearance fall to nothing?

ii

In the above synoptic assessment of what I consider to be some of the most important and influential appropriators of Irigaray, I have predominantly focused on a descriptive approach to these appropriations. What seems to be lacking in my treatment of these figures as well as in their respective readings of Irigaray, is the question of appropriation *per se*. Whether the dominant interest in the appropriation is motivated by a quest for a method, a discourse, a modality of study, or representations of "woman", the question of a founding for these appropriations still remains to be addressed.

As I have attempted to show, most of the appropriators read Irigaray ideologically, a dimension that certainly is at work in her writings. However, in Irigaray's appropriation of Nietzsche as well as in the above mentioned appropriations of her work, the issue of foundation is skirted.

Much of Heidegger's meditation on *Ereignis*[20] attempts to broach this complicated question. In his work *On Time and Being*,

Heidegger deliberates on the privative aspect of what appears, in the sense that there is an absentive component to Being itself and to all beings. *Ereignis* is temporal in its structure and as such it speaks to the presencing and absencing of that which is. Because you cannot say what Being is or what Time is, what presences itself cannot be fully dis-closed. Rather, Being is given, Time is given and the only way we can approach this "givenness", is by awaiting:

> Presence means: the constant abiding that approaches man, reaches him, is extended to him. But what is the source of this extending reach to which the present belongs as presencing, insofar as there is presence? True, man always remains approached by the presencing of something actually present without explicitly heeding presencing itself. But we have to do with absence just as often, that is, constantly. For one thing, there is much that is no longer present in the way we know presencing in the sense of the present. And yet, even that which is no longer present presences immediately in its absence – in the manner of what has been, and still concerns us. What has been does just not vanish from the previous now as does that which is merely past. Rather, what has been presences, but in its own way. In what has been, presencing is extended.[21]

Something is given now, and this something is *Ereignis*. Thus, any kind of process involves a witholding of the past from the future and right now. Witholding is therefore an essential component of "now".[22] For Heidegger, however, *Ereignis* signals the withdrawal as the event of the proper, which is experienced as something that is negative, a *Nichts*. Yet, it is not absolutely nothing. The problem is further complicated by the fact that the original nature of time is still veiled due to the technological appropriation of time and the Aristotelian standard of time thought as a sequential progression. "True time" points instead to the arrival of that which has been, thought as a gathering of essential Being, *before* the given moment:

> For time itself is nothing temporal, no more than it is something that is. It is thus inadmissable to say that future, past and pre-

sent are before us "at the same time". Yet they belong together in the way they offer themselves to one another. Their unifying unity can be determined only by what is their own [*eigen*]; that they offer themselves to one another.[23]

What they offer is nothing other than themselves, that is, the presencing that is given in them. But with this presencing, a time-space opens up. But time in this context does not denote a succession of a sequence of nows. Rather, time-space instead speaks to the "openness which opens up the mutual self-extending of futural approach, past and present".[24] In its foundational nature, this openness provides the primordial space that allows space as we usually know it to unfold. Thus, it is *prespatial*, and as such can make room for space.

In traditional metaphysical language, time-space is thought in terms of the distance measured between two time-points, and as such, it is the result of calculation. However, for Heidegger, true time has nothing to do with calculated time and is not merely three-dimensional in its openness. He adds a fourth dimension:

> But the dimension which we call four in our count is, in the nature of the matter, the first, that is, the giving that determines all. In future, in past, in the present, that giving brings about to each its own presencing, holds them apart thus opened and so holds them toward one another. For this reason we call the first, original, literally incipient extending in which the unity of true time consists "nearing nearness", "nearhood" (*Naheit*), an early word still used by Kant. But it brings future, past and present near to one another by distancing them. For it keeps what has been open by denying its advent as present. This nearing of nearness keeps open the approach coming from the future by withholding the present in the approach. Nearing nearness has the character of denial and withholding. It unifies in advance the ways in which what has-been, what is about to be, and the present reach out toward each other.[25]

Thus, what is being said about the "event of Appropriation" must be thought absolutely negatively. What is here in *Ereignis* is already *not* here. In this sense, it is useless to approach this guiding path of thinking through logic or through technological thinking. *Ereignis* therefore cannot be named, nor transposed into propositional thinking, but can only serve in the service of thought. Writes Heidegger:

> Appropriation is not the encompassing general concept under which Being and time could be subsumed. Logical classifications mean nothing here. For as we think Being itself and follow what is its own, Being proves to be destiny's gift of presence, the gift granted by the giving of time. The gift of presence is the property of Appropriating. Being vanishes in Appropriation. In the phrase "Being as Appropriation", the word "as" now means: Being, letting-presence sent in Appropriating, time extended in Appropriation.[26]

For Heidegger, *Ereignis* is the unique and ultimate *a priori*[27] from whence things might emerge. But, just as you cannot derive the source from the stream, *Ereignis* does not designate another meaning of Being. Rather, it holds together possible meanings of Being, encompassing in it all of identity, comprised of differences. Until this *a priori* has been addressed, beyond any metaphysical notions of space and time that we have, we cannot even start to ask the question of human being. No philosophical discussion can approach *Ereignis*, and, therefore, it is completely useless precisely because it is preparational and foundational.

Heidegger's radical phenomenology cannot be represented, and the word *Ereignis* cannot represent it, since it is only a word for "the unique". But how can something "unique" be? According to Heidegger, time is essential to it. He proposes the contemporaneous of the three possible temporal ecstasies/ex-stasies: first, the past; second, the unfolding of the past in the present (pre-sent, in the sense of a fore-sending and a gift); and third, what is still ahead of us because of this unfolding of the past.[28]

In *Being and Time*,[29] Heidegger furthermore develops this proximity between time and Being in Appropriation when he pursues the essential belonging together of man and Being. Our only possible power lies, according to Heidegger, in death, which signals one's total and definite impotence. However, the sense of one's immanent possible impotence is a power and constitutes all of one's existence as one's *potentiality* for Being.

This power whereby we can sense our mortality is for Heidegger the most uncanny [*Unheimlich*] and the most unique and the most far-reaching power in one's life as power. Through the possibility of death, man senses his ownmost homelessness and his strangeness. At the same time, man can only affirm himself/herself as mortal, which is the most negative experience and which anticipates nothingness. However, its effectiveness is completely positive.

Through the formula of the "possibility of an impossibility", Heidegger establishes the relationship that constitutes all of our instrumentalities and activities. In the anticipation of our own impotence and disappearance lies our utmost affirmation. But language is implicated in this problematic. In technological thinking, a metaphysics of Being has emerged, which enframes and thus constitutes itself as *Gestell*.[30] According to Heidegger, language has become part of this *Gestell*. In Western metaphysics Being has been thought as idea, as *kinesis*, and as *dynamis*, a *Gestell* that is disclosed in saying as speech. In *Ereignis*, Being is appropriated and appears enframed in language:

> Speech understood as the fullness of its meaning transcends – and does so always – the physical-sensible side of phonetics. Language, as sense that is sounded and written, is in itself supra-sensuous, something that constantly transcends the merely sensible. So understood, language is in itself metaphysical.[31]

Just like subjectivity appears in the ear of the other, so language is this otherness. What is heard is what is. However, in order for man to hear *Ereignis*, he has to listen to that which is unspoken in the speaking. Through the enframing [*Gestell*], modern man only hears the information that (s)he can gather from propositional thinking that delivers an object of knowledge to thought. Heidegger, on the other hand, wants language to be delivered to its freedom whereby the appropriating uncovers.

However, in the age of technology, scientific and theoretical agendas demand that language deliver in its enframement. As such, it commands that man be uniformally informed (through, for example, the cybernetic machinery).[32] Language has therefore become formalized and depends on the calculated availability of saying. In our attempt at formalizing language in pursuit of our theories, we have objectified language itself and have made of it another object of study.[33] Heidegger speaks to this impulse in the following:

> In order to be where we are, we human beings remain committed to and within the being of language, and can never step out of it and look at it from somewhere else. Thus we always see the nature of language only to the extent to which language itself has us in view, has appropriated us to it. That we cannot know the nature of language – know it according to the traditional concept of knowledge defined in terms of cognition as representation – is not a defect, however, but rather an advantage by which we are favored with a special realm, that realm where we, who are needed and used to speak language, dwell as *mortals*.[34]

For Heidegger, traditional philosophy cannot get at that which language hides from modern man. As the pre-thematic *a priori*, *Ereignis* cannot appear in theoretical discourse. Instead, according to Heidegger, we have to turn our ears to the sayings of the Pre-Socratics in their thinking on *aletheia*, *logos* and *phusis*. Or, we might follow Plato's advice, and listen to the poets (an advice that Heidegger chooses to follow in his readings of, for instance, Hölderlin, Trakl and Rilke).

In his meditation on "saying" [*logos*], Heidegger never claims to capture it in any of his statements. Only in the silence of the word can the appropriating appear, as the showing movement within the being of language. However, this silence is not captured in a deliberation on silence. Rather, saying resides in Appropriation, as *qua* showing, is the most appropriate mode of appropriating:

For appropriating Saying brings to light all present beings in terms of their properties – it lauds it, that is, allows them into their own, their nature. [...] Language has been called "the house of Being". It is the keeper of being present, in that its coming to light remains entrusted to the appropriating show of Saying. Language is the house of Being because language, as Saying, is the mode of Appropriation.[35]

iii

But what implications can we draw from Heidegger's meditation on *Ereignis* in relation to the above-mentioned feminist appropriations of Irigaray, as well as to my appropriation of these appropriators and of Irigaray? Obviously, they are manifold. First, there is the explicit tendency in all of the above to treat Irigaray's texts as facts which are attributed an unquestionable presence and being, and which therefore are "ready-at-hand" to appropriate and interpret. Lost in this approach is any consideration of how this text appears or what its ontological status is.

In this sense, the empirical unfolding of words on the page are taken to be a testimony for its being. At best, these words are given a polysemic value, which, however, provided we have the appropriate hermeneutical tools, can be deciphered and accounted for. Thus, if the text at any time veils something from our view, it is our conviction that, by using an effective methodology, we can gain access to this hidden material. It is in this context that I understand the privileging of the psychoanalytic model by these appropriators, since it promises to disclose the unconscious dimensions of the text.

Secondly, in all of the above approaches (including my own), language is considered instrumentally, that is, as an object of knowledge that can be represented and which can yield answers to all questions posited. What it fails to acknowledge, however, is that language is our collective dwelling-place, and that we cannot separate ourselves from it. Instead, language speaks us more than we speak it. Thus, language has always already positioned us, in so far as it has us in view, and our being has been both spatially and temporally pre-understood in terms of how these have epochally appeared in language, prior to our individual coming to be in language.[36]

But, what remains hidden from view, is the *Ereignis* that predates all of these occurrences and which in its foundational Being allows all of these epochal presencings of temporal and spatial concepts to be. As Heidegger has pointed out, language has claimed us in a particular way in Appropriation long before we come to language. And, in the wake of Platonism, the memory of this enigmatic way in which we belong to language has been forgotten. We could therefore say that all that is said and done in language – be it our pursuit of "pure reason" or of a different representation of woman – all of these endeavors speak in a certain sameness in relation to the ontological difference that occurs in *Ereignis* as the "event of appropriation".

CHAPTER II:
Theoretical Preliminaries

i

In *Spurs: Nietzsche's Styles*,[1] Jacques Derrida explores the interrelationship between art, style and truth in Nietzsche's writings. For Derrida, this problematic cannot be disassociated from the question of "woman". However, within this problematic, the question of what "woman" is will forever be postponed. Writes Derrida:

> It is impossible to disassociate the questions of art, style and truth from the question of the woman. Nevertheless the question "what is woman?" is itself suspended by the simple formulation of their common problematic. One can no longer seek her, no more than one could search for woman's femininity or female sexuality. And she is certainly not to be found in any of the familiar modes of concept or knowledge. Yet it is impossible to resist looking for her.[2]

Anyone seeking answers to these questions will necessarily be caught in this paradoxical situation. Even if the seeker acknowledges the impossibility of finding answers within the confines of conventional epistemological discourse, he/she cannot resist the compulsion to look for them. When Nietzsche claims that "truth is the lie that we cannot live without", he likens woman to truth. In this sense, Nietzsche embraces "woman"/"truth" as the simulacrum that remains resistant to any determinable identities. Derrida points to this untruth in truth, that is, the divergence within, in the following way:

The divergence within truth elevates itself. It is elevated in quotation marks (the screeching machinations of a hooker, or crane (*grue*), its flight and clapping claws). Nietzsche's writing is compelled to suspend truth between tenter-hooks of quotation marks – and suspended there with truth is – all the rest. Nietzsche's writing is an inscription of the truth. And such an inscription, even if we do not venture so far as to call it the feminine itself, is indeed the feminine "operation". Because woman´ is (her own) writing, style must return to her. In other words, it could be said that if style were a man (much as the penis, according to Freud is the "normal prototype of fetishes"), then writing would be a woman.[3]

Thus, writing becomes the new signature for "woman". But, by putting "woman" in quotation marks, that is, relegating her being to the realm of writing whereby she inscribes/writes herself as a woman-in-effect,[4] Derrida understands *l'opération féminine* solely within the confines of language. For Derrida, *écriture* (writing) is the tracing and marking of difference, an activity which has been repressed and devalued for its fundamental absence in a culture which has privileged unity, coherence and mastery through its notion of "Being as presence".

In his critique of Western metaphysics, Derrida positions the deconstructive strategy as a means to disclose the "phonologo-centric" closure around which our whole conceptual and epistemological framework is constructed. By privileging speech above writing, the Aristotelian *logos* above corporal materiality, and coherent sameness above fragmented difference, we have become enclosed within these hierarchical binary oppositions which form the foundation of our philosophical tradition. Writing (*écriture*), as the *locus* where difference might emerge thus stands at the margins of epistemological discourse, but can never be completely disassociated from it.

Différance thought as the "systematic play of differences, of the traces of differences, of the *spacing* by means of which elements are related to each other",[5] becomes another word for the infinite production of (self)difference, while also incorporating a spacial and temporal positioning. The spacial positioning involves the spacing in writing by which every element depends on the space within itself of the trace of the "other" through which it constitutes itself via difference. Likewise, the temporal positioning involves the tracing of the always-already-there[6] as well as announcing the always-to-become in whatever manifests itself as "present".

Additional terms such as dissemination and deference connote ways in which the process of writing differs from itself. In a simplified vocabulary, one could say that dissemination alludes, among other things, to that which escapes signification or which does not "bear significant fruit", but which instead eludes mastery, return to the same, or teleological control. Deference resembles dissemination in that it undermines any notion of writing as referential or transparent; meaning in writing is deferred, much like the effect of the psychic impulse is postponed and deviated from any conception of linearity.

In fact, Derrida relates his theory of writing to Freud's theory of the unconscious and the dream work.[7] Distortions in the process of signification – produced by mechanisms of displacement, condensation and overdetermination as well as postponement and repetition – all of these phenomena divert the written text away from any sedimentation of meaning. Together they serve to emphasize the Derridean notion of verbal free-play, of expenditure and excess inherent in the very texture of writing.

In *Spurs*, Derrida raises the question of "woman", of *écriture* and the styles of Nietzsche by returning to what he calls "a certain Heideggerian landscape"[8] in order to pursue his interpretation of Nietzsche's texts. However, Derrida admits that in order for his interpretation to take place, there is the Heideggerian reading of Nietzsche that must be accounted for. Heidegger's "mighty tome", *Nietzsche*, thus provides the silent ground on which Derrida's meditations on Nietzsche's styles rests. Furthermore, the question of Nietzsche's style is closely interconnected with the question of interpretation *per se*. For Derrida, the Heideggerian legacy is therefore of such magnitude that it cannot be ignored if one is to pursue rigorously any act of interpretation, be it of Nietzsche's texts or any other text:

In taking the measure of that question, however, there is still the Heideggerian reading of Nietzsche which must be accounted for. Whatever the allowances that have been made for it, whatever the efforts that have been exerted (and for recognizable reasons) in France to conceal, evade or delay its falling due, this account too remains unsettled.

Until now I have often repeated the word *castration* without ever appearing to attach it to a text of Nietzsche. Thus it is that I shall return to it here, proceeding, perhaps somewhat startingly, from the plenums and lacunas, projections and indentations, of a certain Heideggerian landscape. The arguments of Heidegger's mighty tome are much less simple than is generally admitted. It opens, of course, with the problem of the will to power as art and the question of the "grand style".[9]

ii
Interpretation and Understanding

It seems appropriate at this point to evoke Heidegger's meditations on the question of interpretation. Heidegger's thinking on interpretation would automatically implicate both Irigaray as well as myself as an inquiring subject in this problematic. The question becomes: what is it, in effect, that summons us in the interpretative endeavor? According to Heidegger, it is first and foremost language that claims us in *Ereignis*. In *Being and Time*, Heidegger speaks to this problem in his treatment of "Understanding and Interpretation":

> As the appropriation of understanding, the interpretation operates in Being towards a totality of involvements which is already understood – a Being which understands. When something is understood but is still veiled, it becomes unveiled by an act of appropriation, and this is always done under the guidance of point of view, which fixes that with regard to which what is understood is to be interpreted. In every case interpretation is grounded in something we see *in advance* – in a fore-sight.[10]

When an interpretation occurs, what happens is for the most part veiled. Thus, in the traditional dialogical situation, we affirm our propositional subjectivity in an objectifying gesture in the act of interpretation – a process whereby the "other" is appropriated by the subject as something "ready-to-hand". What remains unthought in this approach, is the Being of that which is being interpreted, for instance, the text in front of us. Furthermore, what also continues to be veiled, is the understanding, the *fore-having* which is ontologically necessary for any interpretation to possibly take place. This becomes a problem in any attempt at textual interpretation. Heidegger articulates what happens in the following way:

> If, when one is engaged in a particular concrete kind of interpretation, in the sense of exact textual Interpretation, one likes to appeal to what "stands there", then one finds that what "stands there" in the first instance is nothing other than the obvious undiscussed assumption [Vormeinung] of the person who does the interpreting. In an interpretative approach there lies such an assumption, as that which has been "taken for granted" ["gesetzt"] with the interpretation as such – that is to say, as that which has been presented in our fore-having, our fore-sight, and our fore-conception.[11]

Furthermore, what actually constitutes interpretation, is the that "which is understood in understanding, in our fore-having, and can be made to explicitly stand out *as* such". In Heidegger's words: "the *as* makes up the structure of the explicitness of something that is understood. It constitutes the interpretation."[12]

This brings us into the question of the hermeneutic circle, since, according to Heidegger, "[any] interpretation which is to contribute understanding, must already have understood what is to be understood".[13] For Heidegger, who attempts to think outside the subject-object paradigm in his analytic of *Dasein*, this circle is the expression of the existential fore-structure of Dasein itself, in which is hidden a "positive possibility of the most primordial kind of knowing":

> The circle in understanding belongs to the structure of meaning, and the latter phenomenon is rooted in the existential structure of Dasein – that is, in the understanding which interprets. An

entity for which, as Being-in-the-world, its Being is itself an issue, has ontologically, a circular structure.[14]

The problem involved in any form of propositional, assertive interpretation is further complicated by the fact that assertion is a derivative form of interpretation. By assertion in this context is meant "*a pointing-out which gives something a definite character and which communicates*".[15] Assertion always already implies a fore-having, which is constituted prior to any assertive propositioning. This is what defines its derivative character. Theoretical statements must therefore likewise be thought of as being derivative, since they are grounded in primordial interpretation which occurs in an action of circumspective concern. This interpretation happens prior to any presence of words, but that does not discount the fact that an interpretation has indeed taken place. The moment the assertion gives a definite character to something present-at-hand, when "it says something about it *as* a 'what;' and this 'what' is drawn *from that* which is present-at-hand as such",[16] then this as-structure of interpretation has undergone a modification. The modification has thus changed the "*as*-structure" of circumspective interpretation which reaches out to a totality of involvements of Dasein as Being-in-the-world into the *as* with which presence-at-hand is given a definite character. To mark this decisive difference, Heidegger distinguishes between two forms of interpretation: "the primordial 'as' of an interpretation which understands circumspectively we call the "existential-*hermeneutical* 'as'" in distinction from the "*apophantical* 'as'" of the assertion".[17]

For Heidegger, this difference is intrinsically connected to the problematic of language as "the house of Being". Why is it that in the West, assertive theoretical language in the form of metaphysics has attained a privileged position, a language which is grounded in derivative interpretation? Heidegger attributes this to the structure of *logos* itself and sees as inevitable the modification that occurs whereby the *apophantical "as"* emerges in some form or another.

Re-turning to Pre-Socratic thinkers like Heraclitus, Parmenides and Anaximander,[18] Heidegger attempts to retrieve what has been lost in the development of Occidental thought of this primordial circumspective interpretation in the wake of the emergence of the *apophantical "as"*. It is important to note that Heidegger does not attribute this state of affairs to any flaw that can be accredited to any philosopher or period, but rather finds its source in the "error in Being" that governs the destiny of the meaning of Being. Western languages will thus always already hide the ontological status of the meaning of Being while at the same time the apophantical "as"-structure in the sense of its "whatness" will presence in its epochal character.

However, the destiny of *logos* in the West announces a significant change that has taken place in regard to the way in which the meaning of Being comes to be thought. Heidegger identifies this decisive modification of the "existential-*hermeneutical* 'as'" as taking place already in ancient ontology, and that with Aristotle, *logos* is seen as an entity in the sense of both "synthesis" and "dieresis". But he also claims that "along with the formal structures of 'binding' and 'separating'" – or, more precisely, the unity of these, we should meet the phenomenon. But the problem with Aristotle's understanding of *logos* is articulated by Heidegger as follows:

> If the phenomenon of the "as" remains covered up, and, above all, if its existential source in the hermeneutical "as" is veiled, then Aristotle's phenomenononological approach to the analysis of *logos* collapses to a superficial "theory of judgement", in which judgement becomes binding or separating of representations and concepts.[19]

In the development of Western metaphysics, Aristotle's understanding of *logos* comes to guide subsequent thinking and the Aristotelian "binding and separating" have further evolved into a "relating" whereby judgement gets dissolved logistically into a system of "co-ordination". This again, according to Heidegger, becomes the object of calculus, rather than a theme for ontological interpretation. The culmination of this developmental direction is seen in the phenomenon of the *copula*, which has come to be the standard for any interpretation today.

The far-reaching implications of the above outline of the problems connected to the appropriating event in any interpretation, be it in relation to Heidegger's project, mine or that of Irigaray's, first and foremost demonstrate the difficulties involved in making assumptions as to the Being of the text in question. What actually happens in the interpretative act is that language claims us instead of, as customarily thought, the writing/speaking subject mastering the meaning(s) of the text. What speaks in the interpretation is language itself and the meaning of Being is always already pre-understood and lodged within language, even if it remains hidden from the appropriating subject.

Moreover, the event of appropriation in interpretation speaks of this two-fold movement whereby what is to be understood in the text is not its Being, but rather our own preconceived notions of what its Being is, while at the same time our preconceived notions about the meaning of Being does not belong to ourselves, but rather to language. As a result, our illusions as to the power accredited to an inquiring subject is radically undermined. Language does not belong to any subject, rather, we all belong to it and find our Being in it.

Consequently, when Luce Irigaray inserts herself into the discursive field of the Nietzschean oeuvre, the inquisitive path that she attempts to follow has already been trodden by Derrida and by Heidegger before him. In this sense, the language into which she attempts to position herself has always already determined the destiny of her inquiry. It remains to be decided whether she has already been summoned to language in a particular way, namely in the way which understands Being in terms of the subject–object opposition, or, more specifically, Being understood as a *copula*. Likewise, it should be pointed out that my own re-presentation of Irigaray's project is partly predicated upon an objectification (even in its difference) of her text that is guided by the same problem. Thus, in any interpretation, be it Derrida's, Heidegger's, Irigaray's, or my own, language always already guides the destiny of the inquiry. And in the case when an attempted representation occurs, what has happened is that the existential-hermeneutical "as" has been reduced to an apophantical "as" that remains under the sway of the *copula*. As such, it can only speak to the whatness of the text, and will be oblivious to the question of the meaning of Being. In this derivative form of interpretation, the ontological question as to the Being of the text will necessarily be obscured.

One could object to this claim by saying that deconstruction, in its practice (which is usually what it is reduced to in contemporary appropriations of Derrida), defies simple objectification and seeks instead to probe at the vulnerable points in a text where its own excessiveness resists coherence and identity. Without at this point broaching the complex questions attached to the Being of deconstruction, or, for that matter, the text, suffice it to say that in order to speak to Nietzsche's philosophy, *Ereignis*, or the event of appropriation, has always already occurred. As such, it would necessitate that all of Nietzsche's writing could be subsumed under the category "philosophy", and that Nietzsche would have to be appropriated as a figure to which one has attached a system of thought. Even in an attempt to poke holes at this system, the system will at one point have to have been conceived in its totality in order for the lacks to be identified. It would therefore be my contention that no de-constructive gesture could be possible without an inherent representational gesture, even if this representation is subsequently put under erasure, be it through grammatology or the deconstructive strategy.

iii
The Nihilism Problematic

At this juncture, let us explore the problematic of nihilism within Nietzsche's philosophy of will to power. In Nietzsche's posthumous work, *The Will to Power*[20] he writes: "What does nihilism mean? *That the highest values devaluate themselves.* The aim is lacking; 'why' finds no answer."[21] But, in *Thus Spoke Zarathoustra*,[22] when Zarathoustra descends from the mountains to teach the people his newfound wisdom by announcing that "God is dead", he becomes the laughing-stock of the crowd, who perceives him as a madman. But with this prophetic pronouncement, Zarathoustra becomes the first to recognize and embrace nihilism.

Unfortunately, no sooner had Nietzsche's pronouncement been made, before it was subjected to gross misunderstanding and trivialization by appropriators of his philosophy. This error is most often expressed in the (mis)understanding of nihilism as a *Weltan-*

schauung, that is, as a subjective belief, a dogma, a viewpoint or an ideology to which someone chooses to adhere. This is clearly not what Nietzsche attempted to ponder. For him, nihilism appears, but not as a result of a subjective creation or as a cause of "social distress" or "psychological degeneration". Nietzsche posits that when nihilism "stands at the door", one can only ask: "whence comes this uncanniest of all guests?"[23] Instead of looking for the answer in one of its symptoms, Nietzsche provides the startling answer: "it is in one particular interpretation, the Christian-moral one, that nihilism is rooted."[24]

When attempting to set up the problematic of nihilism, it is imperative to know how to ask about the Being of nihilism. This question is for the most part ignored by providing a descriptive representation of the basic constituents of nihilism. But this description can only speak to the what-ness of nihilism as something "ready-to-hand". What is more important is to attempt to get at the essence of nihilism, which requires, however, a more careful questioning. Heidegger has attempted to do exactly that in his *grand livre* on Nietzsche.

In his fourth volume of his "mighty tome" on Nietzsche, *Nihilism*,[25] Heidegger reads the phenomenon of nihilism in the following way:

> Nietzsche uses nihilism as the name for the historical movement that he was the first to recognize and that already governed the previous century while defining the century to come, the movement whose essential interpretation concentrates in the terse sentence: "God is dead." That is to say, the "Christian God" has lost His power over beings and over the determination of man. "Christian God" also stands for the "transcendent" in general and its various meanings – for "ideals" and "norms", "principles" and "rules", "ends" and "value", which are set "above" the being, in order to give being as a whole a purpose, an order, and – as it is succinctly expressed – "meaning". Nihilism is that historical process whereby the dominance of the "transcendent" becomes null and void, so that all being loses its worth and meaning.[26]

If, by revealing how the "transcendent" is devalued and thus fails to uphold the moral and reason-able universe within which man has previously defined himself, how and on the basis of what can man now understand his existence? Nietzsche provides the answer through his conception of will to power, wherein man finds the imperative to shape his own existence and his own universe through an act of transvaluation:

Insofar as Nietzsche experiences nihilism as the history of the devaluation of the highest values, and thinks the overcoming of nihilism as a countermovement in the form of the revaluation of all previous values, and does so in terms of the expressly acknowledged principle of valuation, he is directly thinking *Being*; that is, beings as such; and in this way he understands nihilism mediately as a history in which something happens with beings as such.[27]

What is at stake in nihilism, is thinking a history in which being as such stands. To say it with Heidegger: "In its own way, the name *nihilism* names the *Being of beings*."[28] As such, Nietzsche's nihilism completes metaphysics, Heidegger asserts. It does not overcome it. Thus, in attempting to think the essence of nihilism, it has to be thought within the parameters of metaphysics, and not as a phenomenon exterior to it.

For Nietzsche, in the age of nihilism, art is worth more than truth, and must be striven for in a rigorously disciplined "grand style". Life thought as a continuous process of becoming in a perpetual movement of self-overcoming and self-creation no longer has to answer to the rules of teleology or aetiology, but can only be affirmed within the confines of perspectival subjectivity of man thought as the artist. Nietzsche gives an account of what has happened in the following:

What has happened, at bottom? The feeling of valuelessness was reached with the realization that the overall character of existence may not be interpreted by means of the concept of "truth". Existence has no goal or end; any comprehensive unity in the plurality of events is lacking: the character of existence is not "true", is *false*. One simply lacks any reason for convincing oneself that there is a *true* world. Briefly: the categories "aim", "unity", "being" which we used to project some value into the world – we *pull out* again; so the world looks *valueless*.[29]

For Nietzsche, nihilism is an inevitable and inescapable phenomenon in the late 19th century. However, nihilism is also ambiguous:

A. Nihilism as a sign of increased power of the spirit: as *active* nihilism.
B. Nihilism as decline and recession of the power of the spirit: as *passive* nihilism.[30]

As such, reactive nihilism can only survive through *ressentiment* and an appeal to the already crumbling moral and legal laws in a desperate attempt to attain will to power. Nietzsche places the priest, the philosopher, the Christian, the Jew, the Buddhist, the socialist, and the feminist within this form of passive nihilism. This weary nihilism is to Nietzsche a sign of weakness that signals that the strength of the spirit has been exhausted:

The will to power appears
a. among the oppressed, among slaves of all kinds, as will to *"freedom"*: merely getting free seems to be the goal (religio-morally: "responsible to one's own conscience alone"; "evangelical freedom", etc.)[31]

Active nihilism, on the other hand, embraces the state of affairs created by nihilism and boldly faces the terror of self-affirmation:

"Nihilism" an ideal of the highest degree of powerfulness of the spirit, the over-richest life – partly destructive, partly ironic.[32]

Zarathoustra, as the teacher of the Overman, is the spiritual embodiment of the will to power and the illustrious proponent of affirmative/active nihilism. By remaining faithful to the earth, Zarathoustra re-values and transvalues that which has been previously devalued. In the projection of a transcendent world outside and beyond the material world, Western metaphysical man has created what Nietzsche calls "despisers of the body", of the earth as well as of life. Platonism in conjunction with Christianity and the moral system that this union created are to be held responsible for this state of affairs, claims Nietzsche. But, like every other moral value system, Christianity ended in nihilism:

"Whither is God," he cried. "I shall tell you. *We have killed him* – you and I. All of us are his murderers. But how have we done this? How were we able to drink up the sea? Who gave us the sponge to wipe away the entire horizon? What did we do when we unchained the earth from its sun?[33]

Will to power as art, as opposed to morality and knowledge, will in its staunch nihilistic stance destroy this degenerate moral system in a celebration of destructive creativity that will allow for illusion, intoxication and multiplicity. But this new ground for existence is founded on the body instead of having a spiritual foundation:

Essential: to start from the body and employ it as a guide. It is the much richer phenomenon, which allows of clearer observation. Belief in the body is better established than belief in the spirit.[34]

However, for Nietzsche, the body does not provide another new foundation for "truth" in the traditional sense of the term. All phenomena, including the body, are subject to will to power and is as such always already caught up in nihilism.

Nihilism, therefore, is the inevitable condition under which modern Western man is destined to live, and Nietzsche envisions nihilism at its most extreme to take the following form:

Let us think this thought in its most terrible form: existence as it is, without meaning or aim, yet recurring inevitably without any finale of nothingness: "*the eternal recurrence*".
    This is the most extreme form of nihilism: the nothing (the "meaningless"), eternally.[35]

When Zarathoustra transvaluates the meaning of the earth, the chtonic meaning of which had previously been devalued, he simultaneously alludes to the figure of the ancient Greek god, Dionysus. In his primordial connection to the earth, Dionysus is the god of intoxication, but also of primordial (tragic) pain. The spirit of music that bespeaks the power of will to power finds its expression in Zarathoustra's singing and dancing on the mountain. This stance should be understood in the context of the following quote:

> The overman is the meaning of the earth. Let your will say: the overman *shall be* the meaning of the earth! I beseech you, my brothers, *remain faithful to the earth*, and do not believe those who speak to you of otherworldly hopes! Poison-mixers are they, whether they know it or not. Despisers of life are they, decaying and poisoned themselves, of whom the earth is weary: so let them go.[36]

Furthermore, it should be placed in conjunction with Nietzsche's emphasis on the struggle between the old Christian metaphysical man who has to be overcome and the dawning of the overman as the force of Becoming. The earth, the body and over-abundant life will come to replace the spirit and the soul, which were previously valued. In the age of the overman, however, to sin against the earth becomes the highest crime. Danger and destruction being his vocation, Zarathoustra destroys this moral definition of man and provides instead a new definition:

> Man is a rope, tied between beast and overman – a rope over an abyss. A dangerous across, a dangerous on-the-way, a danger-ous looking-back, a dangerous shuddering and stopping.
> What is great in man is that he is a bridge and not an end: what can be loved in man is that he is an *overture* and a *going under*.[37]

The question still remains to be determined, however, as to how Nietzsche thinks Being in his meditation on nihilism. In the above, we have attempted to outline the basic constituents of his philoso-phy of will to power in the age of nihilism. The question still stands: how and in what way does Nietzsche think the meaning of Being? Heidegger ponders this question and provides the insight that Nietzsche remains firmly lodged within the confines of metaphysics and therefore does not succeed in overcoming metaphysics. Metaphysics, for Heidegger, is the tradition that thinks the Being of beings as a whole. Nietzsche, in thinking Being as Becoming and thinking will to power in terms of eternal recurrence of the same, does not overcome nihilism – in fact, he completes it.

At this juncture, I would like to include Heidegger's meditations on the problem of valuation as it pertains to the question of subjectivity, and by implication to metaphysics and nihilism. By paying heed to Heidegger's thinking on this problematic as he articulates it in his *Nihilism* volume on Nietzsche, I hope to be able to situate more properly the kinds of questions that have to be raised in relation to Irigaray's quest for a *different* subject *au féminin*.

According to Heidegger, when Nietzsche believes that he has overcome nihilism, he has in fact completed it. With Nietzcsche's positing of "revaluation of all values", he effects a definite shift in value thinking in Western metaphysics. "Revaluation" not only indicates that "all values hitherto" are devalued and fall away, but Nietzsche also signals that the very *place* for previous values disappears. Within this new configuration, Heidegger sees Nietzsche's revaluation as thinking Being for the first time as value. From now on, metaphysics is articulated in terms of value thinking.

This observation becomes a major argument in Heidegger's position of viewing Nietzsche's philosophy as the fulfillment of Western metaphysics. Nietzsche's value thinking not only implies a revaluation of all values, but it also requires a new principle for grounding beings as a whole in a new way. This ground cannot be drawn from any recourse to a transcendent (God, the Good, Idea(l)s), but must be found in *beings* themselves. This leads Heidegger to make the following claim:

> If the essence of metaphysics consists in grounding the truth of being as a whole, then the revaluation of all values, as a grounding of the principle for a new valuation, is itself metaphysics.[38]

Will to power becomes the basic character of being as a whole, which is likewise conceived as the essence of power. Nietzsche establishes a crucial connection between will to power and value thinking when he affirms power as what posits, validates, and justifies values. In this respect, power is power only in so far as it enhances power and recognizes no other worth and value outside of itself nor any end outside of being as a whole.

Thus for Nietzsche, a new essence of man is announced through this new type of man who finds himself challenged with the task of reevaluating all prior values. This new type finds expression in the "Overman", which constitutes the supreme configuration of purest will to power. He is the meaning (the aim) of what alone has being; namely the earth. Heidegger explains:

> The Overman simply leaves the man of traditional values behind, *overtakes* him, and transfers the justification for all laws and the positing of all values to the empowering of power. An act or accomplishment is valid as such only to the extent that it serves to equip, nurture, and enhance will to power.[39]

Heidegger furthermore insists that "nihilism" must be understood within its conjunction with "revaluation of all values", "the will to power", "the eternal recurrence of the same" and "Overman", and within the essential togetherness of these five essential rubrics of Nietzsche's thought. To think nihilism in its manifold truth, means for Heidegger "to think the history of Western metaphysics as the ground of our own history; that is, of future decisions".[40] In this context, Heidegger attempts to ponder Nietzsche's statement that "there is nothing to Being".[41]

Heidegger reveals how Nietzsche's forgetfulness of the question of Being implicates him in Western metaphysics as the process of thought which "thinks the Being of beings", but never thinks Being in its essence. Thus, in its forgetfulness of the ontological difference between Being and beings, Western philosophy has busied itself with categorizing beings without asking on what its ground rests. That "there is nothing to beings" becomes Nietzsche's great discovery, but likewise that "there is nothing to Being" becomes for Heidegger the startling assertion within Nietzsche's writing which is the most worthy of thought.

For Heidegger, the entire history of metaphysics from Plato on is seen as implicated in the history of nihilism. Since Nietzsche understands nihilism purely in terms of valuative thought, and his metaphysics interprets beings as a whole as will to power, the *subjectum* as well as the *object* of metaphysics is will to power (which again provides the essential definition of man). As such, nihilism has to be understood as the history of valuation, be it in the form of positing of the uppermost values, their subsequent devaluation, and finally the revaluation of these values as the new positing of values. Thus nihilism takes on the character of a history. But for Heidegger, this does not mean that it has a history, but that nihilism **is** history:

> In Nietzsche's sense it constitutes the essence of Western history because it co-determines the lawfulness of the fundamental metaphysical position and their relationships. But the fundamental metaphysical positions are the ground and realm of what we know as history. Nihilism determines the historicity of history.[42]

It is important to reiterate Nietzsche's view that the history of metaphysics is tacitly the metaphysics of will to power, appearing as valuative thought. Thus Nietzsche's "revaluation" is in the last instance a rethinking of all determinations of being on the basis of *values*. This means that "being", "purpose", and "truth" are fundamentally values that human beings have projected. However, Nietzsche also calls them "categories of reason", a meaning that, according to Heidegger, was attributed to them by Kant, Fichte, Schelling, and Hegel. "Reason" as used within German idealism is to be understood as the essence of *subjectivity*.

Thus, metaphysics establishes itself as anthropomorphism, that is, as the "formation and apprehension of the world according to man's image".[43] In Nietzsche's valuative thought, being as such is interpreted after the fashion of human Being. And modern metaphysics characteristically attributes a central role to the human subject and appeals to the subjectivity of man. In this context, Heidegger identifies Descartes' statement "ego cogito, ergo sum", "I think, therefore I am", as what initiates the beginning of modern philosophy: the self-consciousness of the human subject who forms the unshakable ground of all certainty. Nietzsche thus merely carries out the final development of Descartes' doctrine. Heidegger makes the following observation:

> If metaphysics is the truth concerning beings as a whole, certainly man too belongs within them. It will even be admitted that man assumes a special role in metaphysics inasmuch as he seeks, develops, grounds, defends, and passes on metaphysical knowledge – and also distorts it.[44]

With the dominance of the subject in the modern age, Heidegger identifies a shift from the traditional guiding question of metaphysics: "What is the being?" to a question about *method*. In this way, the most important question establishes the path along which man has to seek the essence of truth about himself and about his object(s) of knowledge. However, the ground of this new modern age is still to be found in metaphysics. But with Descartes, the specularization of man's salvation finds its ground in "man's liberation in the new freedom of self-assured self-legislation".[45]

Within this new metaphysical system, man himself constitutes the new ground on which his certitude is based. His doctrine *"ego cogito (ergo) sum"* is usually translated as "I think, therefore I am". In Heidegger's reading, however, Descartes' *cogito* is frequently substituted by *percipere*, which connotes "to take possession of a thing, to seize something, in the sense of presenting-to-oneself by way of representing-before-oneself, *representing*".[46]

What this means is that with every "I represent" there occurs a co-representing of the representing I as "something towards which, back to which, and *before* which every represented thing is placed".[47] The subject is thus co-represented and represented "along with" the object, that is, human consciousness is essentially *self-consciousness*:

> The consciousness of things and objects is essentially and in its ground primarily self-consciousness; only as self-consciousness is consciousness of ob-jects possible. For representation as described, the *self* of man is essential as what lies at the very ground. The self is sub-*iectum*.[48]

Descartes lays down the absolute principle of the *subiectum* expressed through *cogito sum*, and as such, it is the determination of Being as representedness. According to Heidegger, Nietzsche does not distance himself from Descartes, but merely fulfills the determinations of the *subiectum* that Descartes laid down. Nietzsche already understood this metaphysically in terms of his positing of the "Overman".

This new principle of the *subiectum* finds its expression through the essence of "subjectivity", which alone defines the essence of the truth of beings, Heidegger says. It now becomes important to determine the *method* or the procedure for securing the truth as certitude, which is then affixed to the essence of subjectivity. Man, as the *subiectum*, now controls the whole of being since he provides the measure for the Being of each being. The subject is "subjective" with respect to its de-limitedness, and as the midpoint of beings as a whole, the subject is "progressing towards limitless representing and reckoning disclosure of beings".[49]

When it comes to distinguishing Nietzsche's thought from that of Descartes, Heidegger emphasizes the necessity to examine carefully Nietzsche's implication in Cartesian subjectivity even when he vehemently opposes Descartes' position. Nietzsche basically refutes subjectivity as a product of metaphysical logic, and understands it as such as a fiction. However, the historical connection between the two thinkers in terms of their sameness is infinitely more important than their differences.

According to Heidegger's reading of the two, Nietzsche's understanding of the subject is definitely modern, that is, he understands it in terms of the human "I". And even though it is now thought as will to power, Nietzsche nevertheless adopts Descartes' position whereby he equates Being with representedness and the latter with truth. But since truth is a lie, representedness only gives semblance of truth, which only serves as a necessary value for will to power. Nietzsche thus interprets *ego cogito* as *ego volo* in the sense of will to power, which is the basic character of beings.

Nietzsche's difference in relation to Descartes is to be found in his understanding of subjectivity in terms of the *body* and not, like Descartes, as conscious thought or the soul. However, in Heidegger's view, this alters nothing in the fundamental metaphysical position determined by Descartes. Thus, Nietzsche's metaphysics is viewed not only as being indebted to Descartes' position historically, but it constitutes a fulfillment of Descartes' metaphysics. As such it fulfills it in terms of representation and consciousness as well as in terms of a transference to the "realm of *appetitus* or drives, and thought absolutely in terms of the physiology of will to power".[50]

Let us return now to Nietzsche's statement that initially inspired Heidegger's decade-long meditation: "there is nothing to Being". In light of the above exposition of the problem of Nietzsche's valuative thought, Heidegger rewrites this phrase so that it reads:

> The nothing in Being itself is sealed in the interpretation of Being as value. It belongs to this sealing that it understands itself as the new "yes" to beings as such in the sense of will to power, that it understands itself as the overcoming of nihilism.[51]

In Heidegger's thinking on the default of Being in Nietzsche's discourse, he does not identify this as an "ill will" on the part of the Nietzschean subject. For him, the *nihil* in Being, which speaks to the essence of nihilism, is not a problematic that originates in the subject, but rather in Being itself:

> The essence of nihilism contains nothing negative in the form of a destructive element that has its seat in human sentiments and circulates abroad in human activities. The essence of nihilism is not at all the affair of man, but a matter of Being itself, and thereby of course also a matter of the *essence* of man, and only in that sequence at the time a human concern. And presumably not merely one among others.[52]

Metaphysics and nihilism, as the inauthenticity in the default of Being in its unconcealment, is the work of human thought. But, the relationship of Being to the essence of man is determined by Being, which also determines that this omission takes place in and through human thought. However, when Nietzsche believes that he can overcome nihilism, he fails to understand that this is not a question that can be controlled by the willing subject:

If we heed the essence of nihilism as an essence of the history of Being itself, then the plan to overcome nihilism becomes superfluous, if by overcoming we mean that man independently subject that history to himself and yoke it to his pure willing. Such overcoming of nihilism is also fallacious in believing that human thought should advance upon the default.[53]

CHAPTER III:
A Lover's Discourse?
Echo And Narcissus Revisited

It is within this problematic of nihilism as it concerns Western metaphysics that Irigaray's inquiry into Nietzsche's philosophy of will to power will be situated. As initially noted, the "why" question of nihilism, as the fundamental question of metaphysics, finds no answer. Nietzsche can only "ruminate" on what has happened and try to assess the implications of this for modern man. The rumination provides the abysmal field of thought in which Irigaray attempts to "graze".

The title of this first section of *Marine Lover: of Friedrich Nietzsche*, "Speaking of Immemorial Waters", addresses Nietzsche's forgetfulness of the sayings of the profound waters that cannot be represented in metaphysical language, but which nevertheless constitute the primordial source for all that is. In her positing of an elemental cosmology of the earth, the sea, the air, and the sun,[1] Irigaray interprets Zarathoustra's flight to the mountains in his search for wisdom as a repression and a denial of the primordial indebtedness of his being to these elements and to the maternal and nocturnal waters. Attempts will be made to determine the multiple meanings that Irigaray attributes to these "seas", which might be preliminarily understood in terms of an originary nurturing force/element, or a "matrix".

In the first paragraph of his first section, Irigaray initiates a lover's discourse between an "I (*je*)" and a "you (*vous/tu*)". According to Irigaray, it was necessary for "all of you (*tous vous*)", to have bereft "me" of eyes and for it to retreat in order for "I" to be able finally to re-turn with an-other gaze. If we were (even if it cannot be done) to attribute any referential identity to the signifier "you" in this part, it would have to point to the chorus of masculine philosophical subjects in language that constitute the canonical speculative system of sameness in the West – a chorus that converges around the figures of Plato, Aristotle, Plotinus, Descartes, Kant, Hegel (and Freud), to name the most prolific ones.[2] Thus, the "you" could be read as referring to this collective effort by Western philosophers to deny gaze, voice, and language to the "I", who has had to exist clandestinely in the shadow of these figures. It is, however, precisely because of its non-being within the metaphysical language that the "I" is now able to emerge and to re-approach them in order to return with an-*other* possibility.

But from whence does this "I" speak? The "I" asserts:

> I was your resonance. Drum. I was merely the drum in you ear sending back to itself its own truth. [...] Today I was this woman, tomorrow that one. But never the woman, who, at the echo, holds herself back. Never the beyond you are listening to right now.[3]

Could this "I" as resonance be understood in the context of Echo as she is portayed in Ovid's *Metamorphoses*? Ovid speaks thus of Echo's nature:

> A nymph whose way of talking was peculiar
> In that she could not start a conversation
> Nor fail to answer other people talking.
> Up to this time Echo still had a body,
> She was not merely a voice. She liked to chatter,
> But had no power of speech except the power
> To answer in the words she had last heard.[4]

If the "I" is that which assures the "you" its own resonance in its sameness, then Echo would be an appropriate figure through which we can understand this "I". Echo's destiny, however, is tragic in that she is intrinsically caught up in a parasitic relationship with an-other's voice. Furthermore, her desire for the un-obtainable and self-loving Narcissus, who claims that "I would die before you get a chance at me", causes her body to shrivel up and to "live" as a disembodied voice for eternity:

"I give you a chance at me," and that was all
She ever said thereafter, spurned and hiding,
Ashamed, in the leafy forests, in lonely caverns.
But still her love clings to her and increases
And grows on suffering; she cannot sleep,
She frets and pines, becomes all gaunt and haggard,
Her body dries and shrivels till voice only
And bones remain, and then is voice only
For the bones are turned to stone. She hides in woods
And no one sees her now along the mountains,
But all may hear her, for her voice is living.[5]

Echo's tragic story may serve to understand the complex problems involved in Irigaray's undertaking. On the one hand, the story might be seen as an exemplification of Irigaray's analysis of the female subject's traditional relationship to language, which could be characterized as a tragic one. On the other hand, however, Echo's story might likewise be read as a warning for Irigaray's own project in that it speaks of an inherent tragic desire on the part of both Echo's amorous pursuits of Narcissus as well as Irigaray's pursuit of Nietzsche.

In an attempt to re-affirm woman's body and her sexuality while refusing to establish an antagonistic relationship between herself and her "beloved", Irigaray woos Nietzsche instead of attacking him. It remains to be seen, however, if this love is in fact a tragic one like that of Echo for Narcissus. Or, might it be that Irigaray has found a strategy whereby she will, both carnally and vocally, be capable of celebrating this new kind of love? If this be true, then another question inevitably emerges as to what the Being of this love could be.

It should be noted, however, that Irigaray has herself alluded to the figure of Echo in her essay "Plato's Hystera" in *Speculum of the Other Woman*. Irigaray resurrects this mythological tale within her deconstruction of Platonic truth, pointing to the fact that "even the voice is taken away from Echo" in this platonic scheme. Plato's *hystera*, which Irigaray understands as the matrix/womb that comes before any denomination of truth, has to remain virginal and mute in order for the self-same pronouncements of the image-makers to ring true:

> The projections of the statufied emblems of men's bodies will be designated by the term truth only if they can be lent voices, *echoes* of the words pronounced by the magicians-image-makers. [...] All of this demands, of course, that both a *paraphragm* and the *back* serve as virginal and mute screens and thus keep the strategies operating successfully.[6]

But to return to Irigaray's initial paragraph, the "I" is also understood as that which assures the vocal mediation between these masculine voices. As such, "I" would constitute an abysmal nothingness that allows mediation to take place as well as providing the invisible air[7] which allows the transmission of sonoric impulses. In each case, however, the function of the "I" is to prevent these narcissistic voices from falling into forgetfulness and to guarantee a truthful resonance and return of the sameness emitted by the "you".

In this silent complicity, the "I" still has to love the "you" in order to remember and to project the movement of its own past/present/future. Thus, only by retaining a lover's proximity can "I" possibly be able to trace the tracks of its own coming-to-be. An-other path for future existence and escape from this state of affairs can therefore only occur through a re-tracing of that which is, namely Western metaphysical discourse as sung by this chorus. But the indifference, or even hate, on the part of this "you" toward any other "I", potentially different from their own, continually stifles its birth. Because this "you" can only turn in the circle of its own sameness and cannot fathom the possibility of a deviation from this circle, anything *other* than itself is expelled and forced *outside*.

However, the "I" is returning from this *other* locus far away, which is located outside the boundary of the circle of the "you". In this re-turn, the "I" will no longer be the echo of the "you" nor its double in reflection. The mirror which the "you" has hitherto attributed to the "I" has now been steeped in "the waters of forgetfulness", from which the "you" has protected itself in order to retain its truthful sameness:

And farther away than the place where you are beginning to be, I have turned back. I have washed off your masks and make up, scrubbed away your multicolored projections and designs, stripped off your veils and wraps that hid the shame of your nudity. I have even had to scrape my woman's flesh clean of the insignia and marks you had etched upon it.[8]

The answer to the previous question starts to take form, that is, from whence does the "I" speak? No longer does it speak from the resonance or the reflected image of the "you". Instead, it claims to have found an-other voice from outside the delimitations of the "you". It remains to be established what empowers this voice to speak and to determine exactly from whence it speaks. If it is located outside of the confines of the traditional subject position as defined by Western philosophy, then where is its locus?

Irigaray gives an indication of the source of this new "I": "All that was left – barely – was a breath, a hint of air and blood that said: I want to live."[9] This nothing(ness) from whence the will to life originates is thought of as elemental: air and blood. In Irigaray's scheme, these fluid elements have the capacity to elude the totalizing de-limitations set by the "you", a totalizing that to her represents death: "As for me, your death seems too base and miserly to satisfy my mobility."[10] Irigaray interrogates this nothing and projects in this questioning a possibility that the nothing could be a source of infinite rebirth and renewal:

Nothing? This whole that always and at every moment was thus becoming new? Nothing? This endless coming into life at each moment? Nothing? This whole that laid by the mantle of long sleep and was reviving all my senses? Nothing, this unfathomable well?[11]

Thus, in the true sense of the word "occident" as the land of the setting sun, Irigaray discovers in Nietzsche the potential for an-other life, for an-other "I" and perhaps an-other language. At this juncture, she presents the following question:

And would the gold of their setting sun help me find the strength to say to them: here is the future, in that past that you never wanted.[12]

There are several possible interpretations that could be suggested in relation to this question. First, this nothing from which Western metaphysics has attempted to protect its edifice signals the limit of its own possibilities. As the "Other" in relation to which it can separate and differentiate itself, be it eternity, death or *le féminin*, the nothing has been construed as that which cannot be included in metaphysics. But it is exactly this nothing(ness) from whence "I" envisions the rebirth of an-other voice, an-other gaze and an-other language.

Second, the quote also announces that Nietzsche, the last philosopher of Western metaphysics, is the one who, at the "end of philosophy", creates Zarathoustra, the overman. Thus, as the philosopher of nihilism, Nietzsche is the last one, the setting sun of Western metaphysics whose figure of Zarathoustra will allow us to find the force in the sayings of his predecessors: "here is the future, the past which you rejected." In the shadow of this golden sun of Western metaphysics, the "I" laughs. Wondering whether or not it is possible to transgress this love of golden death, "I" emerges from the earth, with "enlightened eyes".

At this point, there occurs a shift in the pronoun in the dialogue from *vous* to *tu* in the French text. In the remainder of this section, "Speaking of Immemorial Waters", the "I" addresses this "you (*tu*)", a signifier which in my reading will be connected to the figure of Nietzsche. What seemingly takes place, is a shift from a collective address to an intimate exchange between "I" and "you;" a quasi-dialogue which in fact turns out to be, like most dialogues, a disguised monologue. In the form of an intimate wooing of Nietzsche, the lover's discourse embarks on the difficult journey through the many-splendored paths of Nietzsche's text.

However, in this pronounced intimacy between the "I" and the "you", there is also a questioning of what constitutes identity and difference. In the following passage, the "I" identifies herself with "you" even as she differentiates herself from him:

> Different bodies, that no doubt makes the likeness. For, in the other, how is one to find oneself except by also throwing one's selfsame (*son même*) there? And between you (*tu*) and me, will there not always be this film that keeps us apart?[13]

Traditionally, difference has been understood in metaphysical discourse as dialectically defined, that is, through the act of negation of the "other". What Irigaray proposes, instead, is that the one must and will always be intrinsically included in the other and *vice versa*, as a difference within.[14] This, however, poses a serious threat to what is usually thought of as "identity". Self-identity as it is thought from Plato onwards requires that the one be separate, coherent and free from any contamination by the "other". It is with this concern in mind that we have to approach Irigaray's insistence on the plural nature of the feminine, which embraces difference instead of paranoically shunning it.

Irigaray's attempt to whisper "sweet little nothings" into Nietzsche's ear ought therefore to be understood, as I have previously stressed, in the context of her exploration into the possibility of an-other language. By re-tracing Zarathoustra's odyssey, and in particular the lacunas and dark spots within his search for wisdom, Irigaray draws attention to exactly this nothing from whence the "I" might speak in order to effect a difference. When, according to Irigaray, "you" has deprived "I" of her proper constitutive images, this lack does not only become a prison-house for "you" in that he cannot partake of her images as she partakes of his, but it likewise becomes "I"'s enclosure. The task becomes one in which "I" can make this difference heard within Nietzsche, who, perhaps more than any previous philosopher, is susceptible to this new thinking that emerges from "the bowels of the earth". However, Irigaray's reading simultaneously exposes the limitations within Nietzsche's philosophy, even though it announces a revolutionary break in relation to the previous metaphysical tradition.

Irigaray questions Nietzsche's philosophy of will to power through the figure of the circle. The circle – be it in the form of the sun at noon celebrated by Zarathoustra as the perfect star of illumination, or, in the form of the circle of the serpent around the neck of Zarathoustra's eagle as the symbol of the eternal recurrence of the same, or, finally, in the form of the subject's concentric perspective – signifies for Irigaray Nietzsche's obsession with sameness and consequently a denial of difference. Thus her strategy is to probe into the Being of this circle, which in her view constitutes a paranoic construction on the part of the (masculine) subject. In this way he attempts to differentiate and separate himself from the (M)Other as that which cannot be permitted to exist within his self-created circle. Her reading of Nietzsche focuses upon this nothing, which both constitutes the core as well as that which surrounds this circle, as that which is left unthought. Yet, this nothing is equiprimordial to the circle itself, be it at the interiority of the circle or at the exteriority of it.

According to Irigaray, when Zarathoustra worships the sun as the perfect and illustrious star which in its inevitable setting speaks of the principle of the eternal recurrence of the same, he remains firmly lodged within a specular helioscoptic logic. In so doing, not only does he celebrate the circular perfection of the sun at noon, which provides clarity of vision and illuminates his ideas, but he also affirms the treasures of the night and its darkness that the setting sun brings:

> For that I must descend to the depths, as you do in the evening when you go beyond the sea and still bring light to the underworld, you overrich star.[15]

But for Irigaray, the figure of the setting sun also serves to illustrate the inherent principle of decline, degeneration and finality in the eternal recurrence of the same, the necessary constituent in the procreative process of will to power. The circularity of the sun becomes a metaphor for Nietzsche's appropriating specularity, viewed as a net of entrapment of all that is "other" to it. But, the sun always casts a shadow, even at noon, thus this "other" is necessarily present, even if it falls outside the realm of the appropriating gaze. Likewise, when it is noon for Zarathoustra, it is night at the other side of the earth or in the depth of the seas:

> The sun? Which sun? And why should it hide the sun from us unless it is the same sun that you have taken over as the projector of your circle?[16]

Thus, in its privative presence, both its presence and its absence exist, even though this shadow might exceed Zarathoustra's self-centered perspective:

But this torch, your lamp, makes shadow. Even (*même*) at noon. Even/self (*même*) seeing itself. Your noon leaves in the darkness the other side of the earth, and its inside, and the depths of the sea.[17]

Irigaray views this logic of exclusion as symptomatic of Nietzsche's thinking on the question of difference. That which cannot be appropriated within Zarathoustra's willing subjectivity, falls to nothing. However, this inherent degeneration is celebrated by Nietzsche. Zarathoustra himself, as the last man, will therefore necessarily perish as he teaches the overman as the overcoming of man. For Nietzsche, the differentiating force is the abysmal nothing:

> You fold the membrane between us in your own way. Either it is right up and thrust out, or turns faltering back into yourself. For holes mean only the abyss to you. And the further you project yourself, the farther you fall. There is nothing to stop your penetration outside yourself – nothing either more or less. Unless I am there.[18]

She, on the other hand, resists Nietzsche's penetration. Following in a Derridean vein of thought, Irigaray questions Nietzsche's understanding of the Being of difference. At this juncture, it might be fruitful to evoke Derrida's meditations on the metaphor of the "hymen" in order to elaborate on Irigaray's use of the word "membrane". Derrida makes use of the term in one of his strategic ways of thinking difference. Derrida ponders:

> The hymen, the consummation of differences, the continuity and confusion of coitus, merges with what it seems to be derived from: the hymen as protective screen, the jewel box of virginity, the vaginal partition, the fine, invisible veil which, in front of the hystera, stands *between* the inside and the outside of a woman, and consequently between desire and fulfillment. Neither future nor present, but between the two. It is the hymen that desire dreams of piercing, of bursting, in an act of violence that is (at the same time or somewhere between) love and murder. If either one *did* take place, there would be no hymen. But

neither would there simply be a hymen in (case events go) *no* place. With all the undecidability of its meaning, the hymen only takes place when it doesn't take place, when nothing *really* happens, when there is an all-consuming consummation without violence, or a violence without blows, or a blow without a mark (a margin), etc., when the veil is, *without being*, torn, for example when one is made to die or come laughing.[19]

Without considering the complex philosophic as well as the psychoanalytic implications of the above quote, it is possible to assert that the "hymen", as it is thought by Derrida, makes a connection between the woman's body and the question of difference. Derrida approaches the "hymen" as an opening into Mallarmé's writing and uses it as an analogue for the structure of the text which lights up a space and re-marks a spacing as a nothing or a blank space. As Mallarmé put it: "Man pursues black on white"; or, to paraphrase it – life is to be read in the blank of difference between two lines. As such, writing becomes the dramatization of theatre itself as mime. The stage is that which remains when space comes to double the stage and the miming of miming, that is void of any reference.

Likewise, the "hymen" becomes the name for the fusion of two bodies during the fusion of marriage as a sign which signifies difference. However, the "hymen" also leads to suppression of difference, that is, to a confusion of interior/exterior in the very breaking of that membrane that differentiates them. Furthermore, it is also a fold of mucus membrane which partly closes the orifice of the vagina. Derrida also thinks the "hymen" as an effect of the medium of poetry. As such, it is an operation of undecidability which disseminates and thus sows confusion by emphasizing the silence, the nothing, or, the stasis of that which stands *between*.

The in-between-ness of the "hymen" comes then paradoxically to stand for something that consummates differences in the very marking of it: between male and female or, for that matter, between the "bodies" of Irigaray and Nietzsche. As a figure, it alludes to the continuity and confusion of intercourse and thereby alludes to the veil that stands in-between the inside and the outside of the woman.

Ironically, the "hymen" can only take place when nothing really happens. The fusion becomes an "all-consuming consummation" without rapture, or a mark without a remark that is without being, since it cannot have being without being form. A reflection without penetration is made possible by the double structure of the "hymen". As such, it constitutes a textual mark as re-mark. Derrida speaks of a mime of a mime or of the "hymen" as that which initiates imitation as an endless procedure of copying itself. Its space reduplicates nothing but the miming of mime and refers to nothing. This figuration is for Derrida privative through and through. It is *without being*.

It is with Derrida's remarks in mind that I read Irigaray's attempt to understand the membrane that supposedly demarcates the difference between "I" and "you" in the passage quoted above.[20] When Irigaray posits that which separates the two from each other as that which stands in-between, she sees them not as mutually exclusive, but instead as equally partaking in the space that separates them. For her, however, this space has been appropriated by "you (*tu*)" as the abyss and as death.

Like Irigaray, Derrida acknowledges the impossibility for woman or femininity to emerge within the conventional constraints of epistemolgial discourse, from which woman must by necessity be absent. But in the pregnant space of the *entre*, thought as that locus where the differentiation takes place, Irigaray hears the resonance of the "cave/womb (*antre*)"[21] that is always already anterior to any propositional positioning. Derrida asserts, however, that even if one cannot find woman, femininity or feminine sexuality, one can nevertheless not resist the temptation to seek for her figurations.[22] Again these (con)figurations can only be negative. Through her deconstructive reading of Nietzsche, she is thus able to reveal how "your" projections and appropriations are contingent upon "I"'s presence as nothing, as absence, as death and as the abyss.

When Nietzsche appropriates otherness as death and the abyssal, he also creates God out of this absence, Irigaray argues. In positing this implication, she simultaneously signals how she understands God within the Nietzschean schema. God in this sense comes to stand for Being as the first cause, as that which grants Being to all beings, even if it is thought negatively. In this sense, Nietzsche affirms a negative theology whereby God comes to denote that which is void and empty; it becomes the Nothing.

Even though his problematizing of the question is different from that of Irigaray, Heidegger's analysis of Nietzsche's onto-theology in his *Nihilism* volume seems to coincide with Irigaray's conclusion:

> As an *ontology*, even Nietzsche's metaphysics is *at the same time* theology, although it seems far removed from scholastic metaphysics. The ontology of beings as such thinks *essentia* as will to power. Such ontology thinks the *existentia* of beings as such and as a whole theologically as the eternal recurrence of the same. Such metaphysical theology is of course a negative theology of a peculiar kind. Its negativity is revealed in the expression "God is dead". That is an expression not of atheism but of ontotheology, in that metaphysics in which nihilism proper is fulfilled.[23]

In the Nietzschean schema, if God stands for the "transcendent" as it is thought in metaphysics from Plato onwards, then God is vacuous. Being becomes for Nietzsche synonymous with God, and is likewise thought as a vacuous Nothing. Heidegger's understanding of Being, however, shows how Being is both the emptiest and the most meaningful:

> Being is what is emptiest and at the same time it is abundance, out of which all beings, known and experienced, or unknown and yet to be experienced, are endowed each with the essential form of its own *individual* Being.[24]

Being is the most universal, the most common, and the most said, since in every conjugated verb, Being is always understood. However, even though Being is what is the most reliable in every-day existence, Being cannot provide a ground. Writes Heidegger:

> And yet Being offers no ground and no basis – as beings do – to which we can turn, on which we can build, and to which

we can cling. Being is the rejection [*Ab-sage*] of the role of such grounding; it renounces all grounding, is abyssal [*abgründig*].[25]

Nietzsche's destructive position, within which she understands his flirtation with death and eternity while seemingly transvaluing life and the earth, implies a soliciting of the nothing in a star-gazing, extra-terrestrial search for mastery all the while ignoring the secrets of the earth:

> But if your God dies, how keen is your distress. Endless is your despair and your rage to destroy even the very beginning of this nothingness. The more you seek out the source of danger and strive to control it, the more abyssal is the tomb. Before, when you gazed at the stars, at least you left earth the chance of her secret. Now you dig into the earth to recover something she has taken or withheld from you. But nothing is hidden from you by this ground that keeps your footsteps.[26]

By focusing on death, the nothing and eternity in their so-called celebration of the body, of life and of the earth, Nietzsche's "superior men" seem to flee that which they wish to reevaluate, claims Irigaray. They are on earth, but have no love for it. In fact, Irigaray sees their true passion to be their necrophilic love for death:

> And that your raptures taste of death because you refuse to taste death – this he already knows who beyond your life and your death pursues his way.[27]

By alluding to the following passage in *Thus Spoke Zarathoustra*, "The Seven Seals (or: The Yes and Amen Song)", Irigaray points to Nietzsche's amorous leap into the transcendent realm:

> Never yet have I found the woman from whom I wanted children, unless it be this woman whom I love: for I love you, O eternity.[28]

Nietzsche here affirms eternity as the sole woman lover for him, which for Irigaray indicates that he is departing from the earth. This declaration of love implies a forsaking of the sensuous realm of the body for that of the supra-sensuous. Asks Irigaray:

> But if your only love is for eternity, why stay on this earth? If pleasures and mortifications, for you, are perpetually bound together, why don't you give up living? If birth amounts to a beginning of death, why drag out the agony?[29]

But how does Irigaray in the above quote understand "woman"? If "woman" is here to be understood as that which is deprived of material existence and as a biological, thus empirical entity, then this quote will indeed become crucial. "Woman" as lover, biologically speaking, is then seen as that which Nietzsche shuns. In this sense, he becomes for Irigaray yet another in the army of Western truth-seekers who have excluded living women in search of a "higher love".

Similarly, if "woman" here signifies transcendence in the sense of an other-worldly entity, then Nietzsche can be added to the rest of the line of idealist philosophers who can only think woman as an idealized space. But, finally, if what Nietzsche has in mind by nominating "woman" eternity is another figure through which he understands will to power and eternal recurrence of the same, then it might be contended that "woman" as conceived by Nietzsche in fact is very close to Irigaray's notion of *le féminin*, thought as that procreative nothing from whence everything emerges. The difference that I might point out would be that Nietzsche thinks this nothing destructively as well as productively, whereas Irigaray seems to have reservations when it comes to the destructive aspect of will to power.

Irigaray therefore concludes that the earth and night cannot provide for Zarathoustra anything different from what his day has already provided him. In this sense, the wisdom that the secrets of the night were to reveal, cannot be heard, because he can only hear the *same*:

> And nothing is in store for him at mid-night except what, at his

midday, he stored away. And if mid-night be even darker than his day had imagined, that is the way his star still rises to perfect his circle.[30]

Returning to the figure of the circle, Irigaray introduces the image of the spider to illustrate the concentric edifice that Zarathoustra creates in his appropriation of the universe, including the earth and the night. But, the teacher of the overman becomes caught in his own net, because he is forced to remain within the world that he has created for himself. Furthermore, Irigaray questions the matter from which his thread has been spun. From whence does it come?:

And your last dream is that some spider weaving her web around you is after your blood. For you are caught in her web. And no spider exists but the one you wove to make your circle. And yet you drew the stuff of your web from the womb of a (female) other, did you not?[31]

The problem becomes one of origin. What grants the Being of this circle? Nietzsche's reply would be that will to power grants its Being. Irigaray calls this a circular argument, and the circle is precisely the figure that she attempts to break open. For Irigaray, it is the silence, the absence and the deep immemorial waters that seep through the tightly formed circle and slowly dissolve it that have the capacity to create a rift in this neatly defined circle whereby the Nietzschean subject is capable of appropriating all that is:

The old, deep mid-night to whom one may not speak aloud in the day-time. And whose many voices rise up when the tumult of your heart is still.

And thus the unheard speaks to you, and slips into your nocturnal soul which, this once, is not sleeping. And says: "Oh man! take care."[32]

So when Zarathoustra jumps high and dances around in the mountains, Irigaray sees him as attempting to fly away from these nocturnal voices of a *different* night than the one he has seen illuminated by the sameness of the light of his day. If Zarathoustra is the meaning of the earth, then why does he attempt to fly from it, asks Irigaray? His desire is to take off into eternity, that is, to enter the circle of eternal recurrence, instead of listening to the deep secrets that the earth could provide for him. But in the center of this endless repetitive motion of the circle, there remains a captive, namely *"je:"*

> That, for your eternity, everything should always turn in a circle, and that within that ring I should remain – your booty.[33]

One of the questions at stake in this section, is the question of temporality. Irigaray accuses Nietzsche of freezing time into an endlessly recurring circle of repetition, thus denying the possibility of difference and uniqueness. She claims to propose a different unfolding of time:

> For every hour, in its firstness, its uniqueness, pleases me.
> And when everything starts again, already (I) am gone elsewhere. Whole (I) shall be at every moment, and every whole moment. And he who repeats so that time will come back has already separated himself from time.[34]

The difficult question of temporality in Nietzsche is too complex for us to be able to do justice to at this point. But Irigaray has pointed to a crucial question in what could be defined as Nietzsche's mechanistic view of time. Based on a predominantly 18th and 19th century system of thought, Nietzsche's eternal recurrence of the same might be seen as grounded in a tradition of thought that found its origin in the Newtonian law of gravity. Newton's notion of the solar system as a set of mobile points that are distributed in space governed by the law of gravity informs this mechanistic system. In this conception, time is fully reversible. Irrespective of the direction, the system will remain intact. What is furthermore implied in this kind of system is its perfect perpetual movement. The system operates and depends on time, but it is not its directive.

Irigaray's rethinking of the question of time could be better understood in the context of the change in the notion of time that occurred in the wake of the industrial revolution, namely due to the second law of thermo-dynamics. This law invalidates any possibility of a perpetual motion as in the Nietzschean scheme. Movement is rather seen as one that is directed towards *entropy*, that is, the moment when energy turns back upon itself as a movement toward stillness. Time is now endowed with a specific *direction* that is not reversible. In this conception of time, there is a recovery of much philosophy of first causes, understood in the sense of the Greek *"Kaos"*. It is also possible to detect a drift from difference to dissipation.

In thermo-dynamics,[35] we can differentiate a system that is both isolated and closed. For instance, in reference to the organism, there is both a micro and a macro level of understanding. Within this system, no flow of matter or heat crosses the wall that defines it. If it does, then the system can no longer govern itself. As such, the system has to be a closed one. Thus, we can assert that all of the systems through which time has been thought to date end in closure, be it the mathematical-logical system, the mechanical or the thermo-dynamic system. It is in this context that we can understand Derrida's statement that all traditional methods of thinking close off reading. When you try to open it up, you have to retrace the tradition until you reach the closure.

Thought in this way, it is possible to understand Nietzsche's thinking on nihilism as the path by which he unveils the closure of the mathematical-logical system, while Freud's thermo-dynamic model undermines the existence of the Nietzschean mechanical model. Thus, by implication, Irigaray's reading of Nietzsche's mechanistic notion of time as eternal recurrence of the same follows in the Freudian path of critique of the models that dominated philosophy and science at the time when psychoanalysis was in its infancy.

But, in the following quote from *The Ethics of Sexual Difference*[36], Irigaray attacks Freud's privileging of thermo-dynamics as the scientific model through which sexuality, and by implication time, ought to be thought. In her view, the principles of thermo-dynamics seem to be more isomorphic to masculine male sexuality than to that of the feminine:

Psychoanalytic science is founded on the two first principles of thermodynamics, which uphold the model of the libido according to Freud. Now these two principles appear to be more isomorphic to masculine sexuality than to feminine sexuality. Feminine sexuality being less submissive to alternations of tension-discharge, to the conservation of energy required, to the maintenance of states of equilibrium, to functioning in closed circuits and reopening by saturation, to reversibility of time, etc.[37]

Irigaray seems instead to call for a modification of the thermodynamic model by invoking the work of Prigogine:[38]

Female sexuality harmonizes perhaps better – if it is necessary to evoke a scientific model – with that which Prigogine calls "dissipative" structures. These function through exchange with the exterior world, which proceeds by plateaus of energy and whose order does not amount to a search for equilibrium, but effects instead a traversing of thresholds which corresponds to an overcoming of disorder or of entropy without discharge.[39]

Prigogine's scientific model of "dissipation" suggests for Irigaray a possibility for breaking open the enclosed circularity of the dominant models that have previously dominated scientific as well as philosophical thought. Closeted in Irigaray's argument, I moreover detect remnants of a political discourse of inclusion, as opposed to a Nietzschean notion of exclusiveness and separation. While contesting Freud's privileging of the thermo-dynamic model in conceptualizing the (male) libido, which she claims is still frozen in the figure of the circle of exclusivity, Irigaray not only attempts to provide an-other basis for (feminine) sexuality, but she is likewise engaged in finding another vision on which she can base her "new" conception of time, of love and of existence that is not founded on a logic of the circle and its equilibrium. It is in this context that I read her concern with her "amorous" approach to Nietzsche, an approach that is characterized by inclusion, togetherness and proximity instead of exclusion, separation and distance:

And if your hour ends when mine begins, that gives me no pleasure. For I love to share, whereas you want to keep everything for yourself.[40]

It is paramount for Irigaray to pass *"outre"* or outside the circle in order to decipher a possibility for another economy, another order, or another possibility for thinking Being and Time. Most importantly, however, in Irigaray's proposed modification of thermo-dynamics, is the insistence on a dissipation of sameness, of the self-same, and of identity.

In his *Nihilism* volume, Heidegger approaches the question in the following manner:

> Now, because all being as will to power – that is, as incessant self-overpowering – must be a *continual "becoming"*, and because such "becoming" cannot move "toward an end" *outside* its own "farther and farther", but is ceaselessly caught up in the cyclical increase of power to which it reverts, then being as a whole, too, as this power-conforming becoming, must itself always recur again and bring back the same.[41]

Moreover, when Nietzsche later states that: "To impose upon becoming the character of being – that is the supreme will to power",[42] Heidegger understands him as completing this metaphysical conception of time. Through his conception of Being as Becoming in terms of eternal recurrence of the same, Nietzsche creates a system of constancy in inconstancy.

For Irigaray, the question remains one of a forgetfulness of a memory of the first "female creator (*créatrice*)" that remains hidden in Nietzsche's perpetual self-created circle. In her view it is the resentment of this indebtedness that is the true source of the will to "overcome" and to "surpass". She calls this will to become an illness of man, in which he vomits this "first wet-nurse (*première nourrice*)" from which he has drunk blood and milk. It is in this context that she understands the will to destruction, the will for an eternal recurrence of the same, which for her constitutes a dream of not having been created, and not to be continually created, at each instant, by an-other:

And in your will to destroy, the will to reduce to nothingness anything that might tie you to me by a necessity of first and last hour. To destroy actively what you had to give up in order to be a man. To annihilate the body that gave you life, and that still keeps you living.[43]

The mask-like identity of the Nietzschean subject does not show itself as endless metamorphoses which mimes, at the same time as it annihilates, the movement of natural gestation. Removed from, and different from this production of the subject as artifact, Irigaray posits the elusive (non)appearance of the originary matrix:

Nature cannot be imitated. The mobility of her growth is never fixed in a single form that can serve as template. And is nature's creation not destroyed when one of her moments is taken out and recreated as permanence?[44]

Here, Irigaray uses metamorphoses as a metaphor for the true movement of natural generation. This is a paradoxical statement. On the one hand she asserts that "nature's gestation" cannot be mimed. Yet at the same time she posits metamorphoses as the chosen figure in thinking life and gestation. Are we to understand this within the context of Orphic poetry of de-negation and death, as in Ovid's *Metamorphoses*?[45] Or is it, despite her insistence of the contrary, rather to be approached in terms of a *model* for "natural time"? If it is truly to be thought as a model, then we are surely to treat it as a category that is already infused with meaning(s) and value(s).

However, what unwittingly seems to be at stake here, is the question of the Being of beings, thought as appearance. This problem opens up an inquiry that can lead us into a web of thinkers from Parmenides through Husserl and Heidegger. Without pretending to be able to give a satisfactory exposition of the history of the problem of appearance in its ontological as well as epistemological complexity, all we can do at this point is to recoil in front of this enormous question and to announce some of the implications at work in Irigaray's treatment of the question.

Her polemical intervention is partly connected to what she sees as Nietzsche's adherence to a heliopocentric logic whereby beings are thought in terms of visibility, that is, in their solar specularity. But for Nietzsche, appearances are always already artifacts, that is, always already subjected to interpretation and are as such necessarily removed from the "natural" sphere. Nietzsche's appearances are thus created by the "light" of his artistic subjectivity, which Irigaray sees as his attempt to imitate or parody the natural sun. In this endeavor, what he creates instead, is "a chasm of darkness (*un gouffre d'obscurité*)".[46] According to Irigaray, authentic appearances cannot disclaim their indebtedness to the natural element:

Nothing comes into appearing that has not dwelt originally in the natural element. That has not first taken root in an environment that nourished it undisturbed by any gaze. Shielded from the unveiling of any fixed form.[47]

Irigaray attempts to undermine the privileging of visibility in this specular logic. She questions the primacy of the gaze in the constitution of appearances in Nietzsche's philosophy in particular as well as in Western metaphysics in general, – be it thought as the gaze provided by the natural light of the sun, or, as the artificial interior light of Nietzsche's circular subjectivity.

In her projected elemental cosmology, the "material" is understood specifically as "earth, water, air, and sun". As such, the elemental is thought as a "wet-nurse (*nourrice*)/matrix" that gives life as a gift that is pre-sent, prior to all appearances visibly determined:

Before coming into the light, life is already living. It is germinating long before it responds to your sun's rays.

And obviously, behind every appearance hides an infinite number of others. But, behind all appearances, there remains an irreducible life that cannot be captured by appearance. Unless it withers away.[48]

The dominant metaphor in use in her discourse is that of gestation, that is, of natural child-birth given to a child by a mother. This matrix could also be nominated "mother earth" in this context. In this sense of the elemental, Irigaray seems close to the Roman appropriation of the Greek word for appearance, *phusis*. The Romans translated *phusis* into *natura*, connoting "to be born". Heidegger speaks to this decisive moment in Western metaphysics when the Greek terms were translated into Latin and the subsequent shift that occurred in the thinking of these terms:

> In the age of the earliest and crucial unfolding of Western philosophy among the Greeks, who first raised the authentic question of the essent as such in its entirety, the essent was called *phusis*. This basic Greek word for the essent is customarily translated as "nature". This derives from the Latin translation, *natura*, which properly means "to be born", "birth". But with the Latin translation the original meaning of the Greek word *phusis* is thrust aside, the actual philosophical force of the Greek word is destroyed. This is true not only of the Latin translation of *this* word but of all other Roman translations of the Greek philosophical language. What happened in this translation from the Greek into Latin is not accidental and harmless; it marks the first stage in the process by which we cut ourselves off and alienated ourselves from the original essence of Greek philosophy.[49]

This transformation of the Greek word had then later been taken over by Christianity and the Middle Ages, which constitutes the bridge between ancient Greek philosophy and modern philosophy. As such, the Roman translations have established the foundational ground upon which modern philosophy rests as well as providing the glossaries through which we approach the beginnings of Western philosophy.

We should not underestimate the tremendous impact that this process of translations has had for the destiny of Western metaphysics in general and for Irigaray in particular, who, of course, works within the confines of the Romance language, namely modern French.[50] Thus, in my interpretation of Irigaray's appropriation of *natura* in her conceptualization of the matrix, I read her positing of this (M)Other as conforming to this Roman translation of *phusis* as *natura*.

In his extensive meditation on the Pre-Socratics, Heidegger resurrects the ancient Greek term of *phusis* together with *logos* and *aletheia* when attempting to rethink the question of ontological difference. Heidegger defines ontological difference as follows:

> We speak of the difference between Being and beings. The step back goes to what is unthought, from the difference as such, into what gives us thought. That is the *oblivion* of the difference. The oblivion here to be thought is the veiling of the difference as such, thought in terms of concealment; this veiling has in turn withdrawn itself from the beginning. The oblivion belongs to the difference because the difference belongs to the oblivion. The oblivion does not happen to the difference only afterwards, in consequence of the forgetfulness of human thinking.[51]

It seems to me that what Irigaray attempts to raise through her deconstruction of Nietzsche, is the question of ontological difference, but an ontological difference that is always already marked by sexual difference. Irigaray thus reveals how Nietzsche is forgetful of the veiling that has already taken place of the ground from which the Nietzschean subject emerges. However, Irigaray does not think *phusis* in conjunction with *aletheia* or *logos* in their essential belonging-together, as does Heidegger.

According to Heidegger, the Greeks called the emerging and rising in itself and in all things, *phusis*. However, for the Greeks, their learning what *phusis* is, was not attained through natural phenomena, but rather through a fundamental poetic and intellectual experience of being. It was this poetic and intellectual discovery that allowed them a glimpse into nature in the restricted sense, and not the other way around. Says Heidegger of *phusis*:

> It clears and illuminates, also, that on which and in which man bases his dwelling. We call this ground the *earth*. [...] Earth is that whence the arising brings back and shelters everything that arises without violation. In all things that arise, earth is present as the sheltering agent.[52]

As the process of arising, of emerging from that which is hidden, *phusis* is that whereby the hidden is first made to stand. In this sense, it is closely interconnected with *aletheia*".

However, what remains important to Irigaray in her assessment of Nietzsche, is to point to his (hidden?) *ressentiment* towards the "mother"-figure, which may account for his apparent oblivion of this link/thread to a maternal matrix, necessary for the artist's potentiality of "eternal recurrence". Irigaray poses the question of whether or not Nietzsche's idol of the artifact by necessity originates from the "depths of the seas/mothers *(fond des mers)*". The homophony between *"mer"* (sea/water) and *"mère"* (mother) is evidently at work in this formulation. However, these maternal waters never totally appear in a unique and formed manifestation, and thus can never be subject to representation. Says Irigaray:

> And imitating that was the impossible part of your dream. How is one to mimic something that has no identity? That is fixed in no form. Cannot be encompassed. Eluding capture and catalog, except for the mask – death.[53]

"Mer/Mère" therefore becomes the signifier that undermines Nietzsche's lofty odyssey. Thought in terms of an element that can never be fully present to the Nietzschean specular subject, the nocturnal subterranean waters resist hierarchy, value judgements, differentiation in her obscurities:

> And these surfaces are all equally deep and superficial. Unless one of them is made into a bridge that holds a person up, prevents him from sinking, that crosses over but never penetrates.
> And they all reflect the same (*le même*), if they are found at the same time and place. Which is both necessary and impossible. They move together, but they cover each other over and are never separated from one another.[54]

However, for Irigaray, these waters nevertheless come to stand for some primordial form or *arche*, or origin from whence life emerges, be it of the overman or of the philosopher. Not only does the depth of these waters undermine any attempt at a measured representation, but they also resist light, the privileged element within the Platonic as well as the Nietzschean schemas. These waters create a specular alchemy whereby air that rises from their surfaces solidifies into ice and/or mirror. The specular surface of this ice/mirror is in turn broken when the ice melts into a rippled, fluctuating form. All of these metamorphoses belong to the property of the *mer/mère*. The call of these waters is stronger than any hero's will, but it should not be heard for fear that man might lose sight of his *telos*. While evoking the tragic consequences of the most hardy seafarers as they were met by the sirens' seductive call in Homer's *Odyssey*,[55] Irigaray warns of the dangers that their call may bring to the man of mission. Thus, the ever-curious Odysseus has to be strapped to the mast in order to listen to the sirens' song without jeopardizing his own *telos* or the lives of his men, who in order to shut out this dangerous call must put wax in their ears.

Irrespective of the denial and fear of the dangerous force and pull of this primordial song from the depths of the seas, the waters remain intact and uncorrupted by the trespassers who only want to surmount it "by dint of spurs". In his work on Nietzsche, *Spurs*, Derrida writes:

Thus the style would seem to advance in the manner of a *spur* of sorts (*éperon*). Like the prow, for example, of a sailing vessel, its *rostrum*, the projection of the hip which surges ahead to meet the sea's attack and cleave its hostile surface. Or yet again, and still in nautical terminology, the style might be compared to that rocky point, also called *éperon*, on which the waves break at the harbor's entrance. So, it seems, style also uses its spur (*éperon*) as a means of protection against the terrifying, blinding, mortal threat (of that) which *presents* itself, which obstinately thrusts itself into view. And style thereby protects the presence, the content, the thing itself, meaning, truth – on the condition at least that it should not already (*déjà*) be that gaping chasm which has been deflowered in the unveiling of the difference. Already (*déjà*), such is the name for what has been effaced or subtracted beforehand, but which has nevertheless left behind a mark, a signature which is retracted in that ery thing from which it is withdrawn. Withdrawn from the here and now, the here and now which must be accounted for. But such an operation cannot be simplified, nor can its fine point be honed in a single stroke (*d'un seul coup*).[56]

In Derrida, as in Irigaray, "the spur (*éperon*)" speaks in the forging ahead of the multiple and ever-changing marks/stylettos of styles whereby it embraces and discards various simulations, masquerades, imitations, and parodies in order to create the "grand style". For Derrida, it is in the spurs of these temporary and fleeting artifacts that woman (dis)appears, as that which gives rise to, yet veils the lack of ground that undermines their very beings. "Spurs" thus becomes, on the one hand, the style that protects against the terrifying, blinding and mortal threat of that which appears, precisely in the withdrawal of this (horrific) difference. On the other hand, "the spur" is at the same time the name for the rocky point against which the force of the wave breaks at the entrance of the protected harbor. The always-already-structure[57] that remains hidden becomes, in Irigaray's vocabulary, the abyssal depths of the *mer/mère*. While it threatens to annihilate that which it grants as presence or appearance, it nevertheless leaves its mark in that which appears, as the absence or the withdrawal that is present in any privative presence.

Thus, like the sailboat which glides and forces its ways through the adverse surface of the waters, the mark that is left from its path (dis)appears and is veiled by that which grants its path in the first place. For Irigaray, however, the ship's spur can but penetrate the surface of the waters, and can never reach its profundity. La *mer/mère* remains intact:

> Even as their ships cross over her, yet she remains. The same. Incorruptible. And she laughs as they move onward, seeking the secret of their truth. When they get close to it, they don't notice it. They just keep moving on, in search of something that offers a solid resistance and opposition to their wandering. That offers a rampart to beat back their thought.[58]

In spite of the tireless attempt made by the navigators of the past and the present, la *mer/mère* cannot be reduced to the discourse of truth. Instead, it is by virtue of the enigma that this matrix still holds that human beings may in fact retain the very possibility of a future. The elemental waters is that which in its "truth" resists any appropriations and as such preserves its wholeness:

> But it may be that wholly (*toute entière*) she is not yet theirs. That her mystery remains whole. Has yet to appear to them. Because her ultimate depth does not return to the light of day. And the voice of her abysses is not to be folded and gathered up into a single thought. Rather it (*elle*) will bring down every sail already chartered, if it makes itself heard.[59]

But what is the Being of the elemental, or this abyssal depth of the *mer/mère/*matrix in Irigaray's projected cosmology? Is it an entity endowed with signification, or does it dwell outside the realm of appearances as the always-already structure that gives appearance being? Does Irigaray attempt to think Being in her projection of her elemental cosmology? Is "nature" to be thought as synonymous with matrix/(*nourrice/créatrice*) and as such a word for thinking Being in its ontological difference, but a difference that has always already been marked by sexual difference?

But before approaching these questions in their specificity, let us explore the interrogative ground on which these questions necessarily dwell. What we have to establish, first of all, is how we can reside in the proximity of the question of Being while interrogating Irigaray's elemental cosmology of nature. Heidegger speaks to this problem in his "Letter on Humanism":

> But what "is" above all is Being. Thinking accomplishes the relation of Being to the essence of man. It does not make or cause the relation. Thinking brings this relation to Being solely as something handed over to it from Being. Such offering consists in the fact that thinking Being comes to language. Language is the house of Being.[60]

Thinking, for Heidegger, is an attempt at a reflection that persists in questioning. Contrastingly, by the very use of propositional language, based on causal logic, the premises of our inquiry already imprison our inquiry into the web of what Heidegger nominates as "onto-theological metaphysics:":

> Philosophy is metaphysics. Metaphysics thinks being as a whole – the world, man, God, – with respect to Being, with respect to the belonging together of beings in Being. Metaphysics thinks beings as being in the manner of representational thinking which gives reasons. For since the beginning of philosophy and with that beginning, the Being of beings has showed itself as the ground (*arche, aition*). [...] As the ground, Being brings beings to their actual presencing. The ground shows itself as presence.[61]

For Heidegger, to raise the question of *aletheia*, as unconcealment as such, is not the same as raising the question of truth as it is defined in Western metaphysics from Plato onwards. Heidegger emphasizes instead another meaning of *aletheia*:

> [A]letheia, as opening of presence and presenting in thinking and saying, originally comes under the perspective of *homoiosis* and *adequatio*, that is, the perspective of adequation in the sense of correspondence of representing with what is present.[62]

In her essay on "Plato's *Hystera*" in *Speculum*, Irigaray identifies the workings of *aletheia* in Plato's dialogues as "a necessary denegation between men". She elaborates her observation as follows:

> *Aletheia* will come into play when *denomination* occurs but in fact, silently, it has determined the whole functioning of the language, its terminology, its syntax, its dramatization. Yet this exorbitant power is hidden in the fact that it is *also* used as a metaphor and evoked and recalled. Not without the assistance of a (de)negation: the word is: *a-letheia*.[63]

For Irigaray, this formality which determines all logic and affirmative discourse by means of de-negation has never been questioned. In the Platonic scheme, the mimetic process by which representations appear can only happen through the workings of *aletheia*, that is, the unconcealment that conceals. For Plato, what *aletheia* conceals is the fact that the appearance (*parousia*) is but a copy of the one, *eidos*, the permanent, the identical, or, Being. According to Irigaray, this contention that all appearances only come to be through this process of de-negation still ensures the essential *sameness* in all appearances and does not undermine the integrity of this sameness, but instead solidifies it:

> nothing can be named as "beings" except those same things which all the same men see in the same way in a setup that does not allow them to see other things and which they will designate by the same names, on the basis of the conversation between them. Whichever way up you turn these premises, you always come back to *sameness*.[64]

In her reading of Plato, Irigaray reveals the way in which *aletheia* becomes the *modus operandi* whereby the "veils of oblivion, error and mendacity" are theoretically lifted. In this uncovering, what is being revealed is the fact that every representation in their denegation, necessarily repeats that which tacitly determines them. However, for Irigaray, "their function as *simulations* will itself never be unveiled as *cause*, even, or especially, if it is designated by the term *unveiling*".[65]

Both Heidegger and Irigaray here point to the Platonic understanding of *aletheia* as *homoisis* and *adequatio*, or correspondence. However, most of Heidegger's meditation on the essential belonging together of *aletheia*, *logos* and *phusis* attempts to retrieve a Pre-Socratic thinking in which the three words are thought in their essential belonging together. Heidegger does not accredit the fact that *aletheia* appears to man's experience and speaking only as correctness and dependability to carelessness in human thinking. Rather, he claims that self-concealing, *lethe*, belongs to *a-letheia*.

Furthermore, Heidegger observes that "only what *aletheia* as opening grants is experienced and thought, not what it is as such".[66] Just as *aletheia* has been appropriated as correctness and dependability (in representation), so *logos* has been appropriated in metaphysics as *ratio*, as the measure or the logical in the sense of what is consistent:

> In each case, *Logia* is the totality of a nexus of grounds accounted for, within which nexus the objects of the sciences are represented in respect of their ground, that is, are conceived.[67]

In this sense of *logos*, the ground is thought as the original matter of thinking, that is, as a first cause:

> the *causa prima* that corresponds to the reason-giving path back to the *ultima ratio*, the final accounting. The Being of beings is represented fundamentally, in the sense of the ground, only as *causa sui*. This is the metaphysical concept of God. Metaphysics must think in the direction of the deity because the matter of thinking is Being; but Being is in being as ground in diverse ways: as *logos, heipokeimenon*, as substance, as subject.[68]

Plato and all of onto-theological metaphysics have thought *logos* in this sense, including Kant, Hegel and Nietzsche. Our task will therefore be to ask the following question: is Irigaray's thinking on the (M)Other inevitably lodged within this confinement or does Irigaray perhaps attempt to follow Heidegger's Pre-Socratic path? There are certainly expressed intentions on the part of Irigaray that she would like to incorporate this Pre-Socratic heritage into her elemental thinking:

> I wanted to create from the beginning a sort of tetralogy which would approach the problem of the four elements: water, air, fire, earth, applied to the philosophers closest to us, and also implicate the philosophical tradition, more specifically, from the viewpoint of the feminine. It is necessary to interrogate that which, in a Pre-Socratic tradition, has been repressed, censured, or forgotten, of the elemental.[69]

However, *logos* as thought by the Pre-Socratics, speaks to another aspect in which Being gives itself. Through a meditation on Heraclitus' Fragment B 50 on the "Logos",[70] Heidegger reveals a more paradoxical understanding of *logos*. Heraclitus thought of Being, in its ontological difference of *perdurance* as the manner in which Being has cleared itself as *logos*, as the ground. However, Being becomes present as *logos* in the sense of ground in a twofold way. On the one hand it is the unifying One in the sense of the all-highest, that is, Zeus. As such, it gathers everything into the universal. On the other hand, *logos* also contains within itself, as Irigaray has noted in the above, the essential origin of the character of all language, and in that way determines the manner of utterance as a logical way.

"Logos as letting something be seen in its togetherness with something, that is, letting it be seen *as* something, speaks to its apophantical signification. As initially noted, under the discussion of understanding and interpretation,[71] this *as*-structure which is an important component of *logos*, is, however, not exhaustive in terms of its potentiality. *Logos*, in its apophantical nature also takes over the possibility of covering up. In the secondary phenomenon of *logos* as truth, defined logically as judgement or reason or relatedness, what remains hidden and covered up is the withdrawal of Being:

> ... that which remains *hidden* in an egregious sense, or which relapses and gets *covered up* again, or which shows itself only *"in disguise"*, is not just this entity or that, but rather the *Being* of entities, as our previous observations have shown. This Being can be covered up so extensively that it becomes forgotten and no question arises about it or about its meaning.[72]

For Heidegger, all disclosure releases what is present from concealment. In that sense, disclosure needs concealment, and "*logos is in itself and at the same time* a revealing and a concealing".[73]

The question still remains: what is the Being of Irigaray's notion of the matrix/(M)Other and her positing of the *mer/mère* as the forgotten ground of all appearance? Does she align herself with the Heideggerian inquiry and thus try to retrieve the Pre-Socratic thinking on the *logos*, *aletheia* and *phusis*? Or, does she instead remain trapped within a metaphysical understanding of appearance that grounds itself on the Latin appropriation of the Greeks and thus understand *mer/mère* in the sense of *natura*? Furthermore, does this Latin notion of *natura* in turn serve as the (hidden/unspoken) presupposition for her appropriation of *mère/mer* as the forgotten always-already structure on which the Nietzschean edifice must by necessity be grounded?

There is an insistence in Irigaray on the question of birth as an event that cannot be surpassed or transvalued. According to her reading of Nietzsche, the overman has yet to start living, a claim that she substantiates in his denial of the truth of birth. In her critique of Nietzsche's affirmation of the self as a self-created entity, Irigaray posits that any existence of a body or a self is by necessity always indebted to the (M)Other. In her view, the eternal recurrence of the same thus constitutes an attempt to skip the necessity of material birth. The silence which surrounds this problem creates a hole in the Nietzschean circle:

> Incapable of bringing yourself into the world, you hated the one that gave you life, didn't you? And you reduced to nothing that power that holds aloof from your art? And made death out of your native life.[74]

In Nietzsche, birth is reduced to the nothing. At the same time, birth must be overcome. The thought of being immersed in the "first matter (*matière première*)" is what fuels Nietzsche's anxiety, claims Irigaray. It is precisely this angst which can account for the absence of a maternal discourse:

> Birth. La naissance. La Naissance? La? Naissance? And what if that (*ça*) didn't mean anything in your language? If that/the id meant nothing, in your language?
>
> Birth? An abstract phenomenon assumed by anyone coming into existence. A dead skin imperceptibly wrapping anyone that has just come into appearing. A proper noun permanently covering over anyone who enters into his becoming. A deceit to be worn through every change. An airy hiding place that encircles all becoming in its veil.[75]

This quote might suggest that Irigaray thinks *mer/mère* as that which gives birth, that is, as *natura* in the Latin sense of the word. On the other hand, the very fact that it has been silenced and as such cannot be spoken in the language of will to power, suggests that there is a *logos* that hearkens to that which *is not* in metaphysical language from Plato and onwards. In this sense, Irigaray might be closer to a Heideggerian inquiry than what is customarily thought. Even though the following quote evokes a biologistic discourse, it might be read as an attempt at invoking the question of ontological difference as Heidegger thinks it in terms of *logos*, *aletheia* and *phusis*:

> Where does difference begin? Where is it (elle)? Where am I? And how can one face something that hides from appearing? How can one master that dark place where you find birth? Where you begin to be?[76]

Might we here detect a suggestion of an *aletheic* understanding of appearence, whereby the withdrawal in the very presencing of appearance connotes that which cannot be thought, namely the (M)Other?

It becomes paramount for us to investigate, however, whether this is seen by Irigaray as a withdrawal that is willed and thus intended by the Nietzschean subject, or, whether this withdrawal must instead be understood, as does Heidegger, in terms of the problematic of nihilism in Western metaphysics. Heidegger articulates the problem in the following way:

> Thus matters stand with the concealment of Being in such a way that the concealment conceals itself in itself. The staying away of Being is itself *this very default*. Being is not segregated somewhere off by itself, nor does it also keep away; rather, the default of Being as such is Being itself. In its default Being veils itself, which is the way Being itself essentially occurs in default, is the nothing in Being itself.[77]

For Heidegger, nihilism names the *nihil* as it applies to Being itself. In its application, it is thought as what happens in the history of Being itself, whereby what essentially occurs in the history is determined by Being itself, and not by a subject. The essence of nihilism is therefore for Heidegger Being itself in default of its unconcealment, a default that Being itself **is**.

The question then presents itself: if Irigaray understands this withdrawal of the (M)Other in terms of a subjective problematic, does she therefore envisage that this defective subject can be perfected by letting a *different* subject speak, which would then bring to language that which has been forgotten? Or, does she instead appropriate the Heideggerian meditation on the Pre-Socratic word *aletheia*, *phusis* and *logos* in order to reveal how Nietzsche's philosophy of will to power is implicated in the forgetfulness of the (M)Other in Western metaphysics.

In either case, however, Irigaray has already equated Being with the (M)Other or the *mer/mère*/matrix. This constitutes a major problem in itself. Even though, as Irigaray has pointed out, the (M)Other only figures in Western metaphysics as the nothing, absence, the abyss or death, – does that mean that we can equate this with Being as it is thought by Heidegger? I think not. When Heidegger ponders Nietzsche's pronouncement that "there is nothing to Being" in metaphysics, this means that Being is thought in terms of beings, and that the meaning of Being has been forgotten. Irigaray understands the (M)Other in terms of elemental beings, that is, as the earth, the sun, air and the sea, or, more specifically, the immemorial waters. This implies that this elemental ground is metaphysical through and through, since for Heidegger, metaphysics thinks Being in terms of beings.

Irigaray reads Nietzsche's preoccupation with overcoming as his resentment against this primordial space. His annihilating hatred is targeted against these deep waters of his own coming-to-be. Believing that he has elevated himself beyond the immemorial waters and the contamination that they bring, Zarathoustra characteristically incarcerates himself in the horizon of the self-same circle which he has created.

But in this murder of the Other, has there not simultaneously occurred an abolition of the other, asks Irigaray. Confined within the limits of specular self-redoubling, Zarathoustra suppresses the self-differing effects of his own intentions. She continues:

For, in the other, you are changed. Become other, and without recurrence. It is up to her to perpetuate your becoming, to give it back to you or not, variously deformed. A trace of your passage into her leaves a mark, in the flesh. That forever escapes you.[78]

Even though Zarathoustra embraces the inevitable self-differing flux of the artifact or fiction that is called the self, and thereby welcomes a certain loss of identity, Irigaray nevertheless sees him as demanding the self-identical in the eternal recurrence of the same, a sameness through which she interprets the privileged figures in Zarathoustra's world:

Like a snake that endlessly enfolds the one on the edge formed or projected by its desire. Or a sun, whose rays might conceivably bring back to their focus the illumination of all things. Or the man who brings back into himself the ecstasies of his will, and projects his strength, his tension, his energy, his seed ... only so that he can possess the effects of those gifts and find fresh nourishment, and new growth in them. A new birth, or a survival.[79]

How does Irigaray envisage that this difference should be spoken? What will be the implications for Nietzsche's project if this silence/absence/nothing were to come to language? By outlining the last part of "Speaking of Immemorial Waters", an attempt will be made to answer these questions. However, in so doing, we will venture to pay heed to the above questions, namely whether or not Irigaray ultimately understands this withdrawal from language as a result of the "ill will" on the part of the Nietzschean subject and/or the choir of Western metaphysical figures from Plato onwards. Or, does she instead understand this in terms of the "history of an error", to which Derrida refers in his work on Nietzsche,[80] which ultimately accounts for nihilism as the default in Being that has characterized the history of Being since the destining that occurred at the dawn of Western metaphysics.

In a six-part conclusion to "Speaking of Immemorial Waters", respectively introduced by "For expressing (*La dire*), Irigaray interrogates what the implications of this "last thought", which Nietzsche is not capable of thinking, would be were they to be effected in language. Read grammatically, *La dire* is composed of a noun, *dire*, denoting a language, (perhaps a saying in the Pre-Socratic sense of *logos*) with its determinate article *La*, which would indicate that this noun has been determined or marked by the feminine. In this interpretation, does Irigaray's phrase suggest the arrival of a new language, perhaps without the previous withdrawal, that is, some language of fullness or of inclusion as opposed to Nietzsche's discourse of exclusion and oblivion? Let us first try to listen to what might be heard in her perhaps most poetic section, *La dire*.

The polysemy of the phrase might on the one hand suggest that *La* functions as a direct object whereas *dire* functions as a verb without a subject. *La* could then be read as that which is present/given in the act of speaking as the forgotten memories of these immemorial waters, and as such would be marked by the (M)Other/*mer*/matrix/feminine. The absence of a subject would in this context be of great significance, since in some way it would imply that Irigaray attempts to eliminate the subjective position altogether, and her strategy would therefore have to be seen as eluding the subjective paradigm completely.

First, Irigaray ponders whether or not "speaking (in the feminine)" would affect the way in which difference is constituted. In Margaret Whitford's excellent reading of Irigaray in her book, *Luce Irigaray: Philosophy in the Feminine*,[81] she uses the term "the other of the other" for this new Irigarayan difference. This other difference, which would no longer be confined to a mimetic reflection, (in Whitford's terminology, "the other of the same"), might have the potentiality to break open the circle of sameness. Thus, it would be susceptible to "the play of chance and necessity".

Second, Irigaray asks if "speaking in the feminine" might not in fact entail a breaking open of the ring (of eternal recurrence of the same) in which the (masculine Nietzschean) subject stands, "thus stripping it of matter, form, substance, end, power ...".[82] It would then be robbed of its chance at communicable stability, and nothing, except an empty frozen mask, deprived of its connection with a continuous resource in the living, would remain.

Third, "for expressing it (*la dire*) would require new means for translation, which, she claims, Nietzsche's language lacked. By choosing the mask, which is limited to the frozen appearance of a moment, and therefore incapable of capturing the "flux and metamorphoses of time", Nietzsche favors Apollo over Dionysus (cf. *The Birth of Tragedy*) as well as interpretation over "the movement of life".

Fourth, *la dire* – was that not what Nietzsche ultimately strove for, but fáiled to accomplish, asks Irigaray. And even if he would have succeeded in bringing *le féminin* to language, would there have been interlocutors capable of hearing this kind of speech? Irigaray asks if Nietzsche did not (unwittingly) foresee the necessity for a future deconstructive pose *au féminin*, a pose from which Irigaray establishes her own reading strategy in relation to Nietzsche's text.

Even though Nietzsche most probably would have resented such an outcome of his thinking, he was not empowered to control the effects of his own thought. According to Irigaray, it is doubtful that he would have embraced any future thinking that did not include his own solitary will as an indispensable prologue. By the same logic, he would not have condoned her reading of "Nietzsche".

Speaking *au féminin* would surely mean, by re-enacting them as well as playing around with Nietzsche's projective mechanisms, a going beyond. But once their foundations have been removed, what happens is that Nietzsche's projections come back to haunt him. In his projective will to become Dionysos, Nietzsche (unwittingly) inhabits the mask of the Crucified:

And, as an end, you serve as foundation for the images, the figure, the role, that you unremittingly laid down in your active project. Having passively become the mask of Christ. The realization of your destiny?[83]

But are the two figures really different, asks Irigaray. In her reading they "have the same birth within [his] universe"[84] and are of the same gender and type. Nietzsche thus failed to search deep enough for difference, and his projections of Dionysos and the

Crucified are but "sham phony contradictions" and products of a subjective error whereby Nietzsche failed to recognize the (un)true origin of his own *ressentiment*.

Finally, *La dire* – How? For was not Nietzsche already immersed in the gap between his projected figures and his speech? In this breach, from which his agonizing screams emerge, Nietzsche is bereft of language (as is his other *au féminin*). The abyssal rupture that exists between the world of yesterday and the world of today cannot be overcome. Except by a feminine operation. Nietzsche has become this character, who wants to embrace this other, whether he encounters her in the figure of Ariadne, Diotema (or, for that matter, Lou Andreas-Salomé).[85] He wants to marry her, to chain her to him and his project, as the guardian of his household. But she refuses.

After having been jilted, Nietzsche searches for an equilibrium, which he finds in the eternal recurrence of the same. But the autological movement of the circle of the eternal recurrence cannot be reopened. Thus, he is forced to give himself a center, where the other no longer plays the part of counterbalance or beam between himself and "himself". He is incapable of escaping from his circle, and at that moment, he dies, when the oeuvre is perfected. All he has to achieve at this point, is to sur-vive.

While keeping in mind Irigaray's six-fold "echo" of Nietzsche's thinking as it concerns the possibility of *La dire*, let us retrieve the question initially posed as to Irigaray's understanding of the withdrawal of *mer/mère* from this discourse. I would like to focus on two instances in which I believe Irigaray commits herself to a certain understanding of the problem.

In the fourth part of her outline, she poses the following question: "Was this not the death plot which cannot hold beyond the specific instant?"[86] The question occurs in the midst of a discussion of a possible re-entry of "her" into "his" world. Only by submitting herself to preservation and enhancement of "his" future, for which she expends her energy while depleting the resources needed for her own growth, can she hope to take part in his economy. The quote suggests that a conspiracy of death has taken place. Even though the culprit of this crime is not expressly named, it is implied that the conspiracy has been plotted by them, that is,

Nietzsche and his philosophical complices. This interpretation furthermore suggests that this conspiracy of death has been collectively caused by the masculine subject through an act of "ill will", whereby "she" has been systematically excluded, denied, repressed and forgotten.

Moreover, in the fifth part of her concluding observation, Irigaray writes:

> But were Dionysos and the Crucified One really different? Did they not, secretly, have the same birth within your universe? If so, you would have engaged and sought to overcome only a sham phony contradiction – one created by a subjective error.[87]

My intervention concentrates on the contention that the contrived will to overcome the contradiction between the two was created by a *subjective* error. In my reading, Irigaray here identifies the problem as one originating in a defect connected to the subject. Both Dionysos and the Crucified deny the maternal element; Dionysos by his birth from Zeus' thigh and Christ by his birth inseminated by the Holy Ghost (which is always to be understood within the masculine triad of the Father, the Son and the Holy Ghost). What this entails, is that this denial or oblivion of the *mer/ mère* has been created by a subjective error that has willfully intended to exclude this indebtedness to the maternal. Nietzsche has therefore not properly understood the true origin of his own birth or of his own resentment. For Irigaray, the *mer/mère* is what is left unthought in Nietzsche.

The sayings, that is, the *dire* of this primordial locus *La* in the sense of a "thereness" that cannot be seen or heard, thus makes us reminiscent of the initial analogy suggested between Irigaray/Nietzsche and Echo/Narcissus. *La*'s voice is forever trapped in the echo of the other, that is, of Narcissus. The truth of her voice cannot be heard – it has been withdrawn. Narcissus characteristically withers away in his desire to consummate the union with his own mirror image. However, as Ovid points out, the process of metamorphoses will eventually seize him, and time intervenes to effect his death and thus to transform him into a flower. Narcissus has therefore been subjected to the destructive powers of necessity and chance, and his desire to freeze his image against the forces of temporality has therefore proven futile.

Likewise, we can in this context read Irigaray's orphic logic whereby she reveals the impossibility inherent in Nietzsche's projected sameness and permanence in "eternal recurrence of the same". When confronted with the destructive powers of the *mer/mère*, which governs the process of metamorphoses, the artificial masks of the overman's simulated identities dissolve, like the mirror image of Narcissus.

The crucial question seems thus to have found an answer. According to Irigaray, the state of affairs whereby the *mer/mère* has withdrawn from Nietzsche's discourse can be found in the collective conspiracy of death and in a "subjective error". Furthermore, Irigaray posits in the following the strategy by which will she bring about a change:

> Was it left for her to interpret? To try to undo the work in its last pose? To invent a different relation to the same and the other? That deconcentrates the circle and permits an as yet unencountered play in the relationship? Other music, other graphics, other plastic art of hymen – and within language too.[88]

The task at hand becomes one of interpretation. This interpretation will have to attempt to undo the philosophical oeuvre in its last posture, the Nietzschean stature, as the work of the "last philosopher". All of the verbs attached to this interpretation, "invent (*inventer*)", "undo (*défaire*)", "decentralize (*déconcentrer*)" and "create (*créer*)" are all active verbs that require a subjective agent. This interpretation will, however, have to call for an-other morphologic of difference in language that might hearken the "immemorial waters" of the *mer/mère*.

In her negative stance, "she" has always represented the limit of philosophical discourse. Her figuration as absence, death and the abyss has furthermore been predicated on the forgetfulness of the withdrawal of the *mer/mère*. Within these paradigms, every theory of the subject has always already been marked by the masculine. Irigaray explains:

We can assume that every theory of the subject has always been appropriated by the "masculine". When she submits to (such a) theory, woman fails to realize that she is renouncing the specificity of her own relationship to the imaginary. Subjecting herself to objectivization in discourse – by being "female". Re-objectivizing her own self whenever she claims to identify herself "as" a masculine subject. A "subject" that would research itself as lost (maternal-feminine) "object"?[89]

Without delving into a psychoanalytic problematic at this point, it is necessary to retrieve Irigaray's indebtedness to psychoanalytic theory in her proposed thesis that every theory of the subject has always already been marked by the masculine. Understood in this claim is the Lacanian psychoanalytic notion that the subject is constructed in language. Furthermore, according to her reading of the philosophical tradition, this so-called universal subject has a morpho-logical similitude to the masculine sexual organ. In its symbolic figuration, the phallus is characterized by unity, (visible) form, identity, erection etc.

However, this morpho-logic does not *translate* the feminine sexual organ, which is always multiple, and can therefore only be represented in this masculine discourse as absence, or, as a "hole".[90] It is therefore impossible to capture this plurality in a discourse of unity. By using the example of the female sexual organ as that which has both an inside and an outside, visible and invisible parts as well as a double layer of lips that are always more than one, Irigaray develops her argument that the "feminine" would require a *different* language in order to speak.

The problem is, however, that the language that she envisages would still remain operative within a subjective paradigm. For her, the imaginary, or the mirror phase as it is theorized by Lacan, constitutes a necessary prerequisite for the subject to construct itself. Irigaray claims that one of the reasons the feminine is not present in Western discourse is that the female subject has been deprived of her own "imaginary". By being trapped within the mirror-image of the (visible) unity of the masculine subject, she has been alienated from her specificity that could not be captured within this restrictive specular image. That which is not, that is, the invisible vagina, has been repressed as has all that which exceeds the limits of this mirror. Based on this observation, Irigaray claims that women do not have an unconscious, but they **are** the unconscious.[91]

Nietzsche's subjective projections would of course be implicated in this problem. But how, within her own projections, can this situation be remedied? Irigaray outlines the task at hand, the task of subjective re-interpretation:

> It is true that it would require a revolution in thinking as well as in ethics in order for the work of sexual difference to take place. Everything remains to be interpreted in the relationship between the subject and discourse, the subject and the world, the subject and the cosmic, and the micro and the macrocosm.[92]

But the question arises: What difference can be identified in Irigaray's theorizing on the possibility of a *different* subject from Nietzsche's re-evaluating subject? They certainly embrace different values, but what they have in common, is the emphasis on re-interpretation and re-valuation as a principle of affirming their subjectivity.[93]

If we reenter Irigaray's quest for a *different* subject onto this arena, it becomes evident that her understanding of the subject coincides to a great extent with that of Nietzsche. Even though she points to the forgetfulness of *mer/mère* as the primordial ground for the Nietzschean subject, and as such reveals the overman's willing concentric subjectivity, she fails to see this as a problem connected to nihilism. In fact, the word nihilism never appears in her treatment of Nietzsche's *Thus Spoke Zarathoustra*.

Part of the reason for her blindness when it comes to the question of nihilism, is to be found in her own inadequate treatment of the question of Being. As previously demonstrated, her understanding of Being, which is equated with *mer/mère*, is metaphysical through and through. Defined within her elemental cosmology, Being comes to stand for the earth, the sun, the sea and the air. In short, they become *values* that must be posited to devalue prior values, including those of Nietzsche, who only seemingly places any worth on the mater-ial. Furthermore, by valuing a logic of fluidity as opposed to the previous valuation of solidity, Irigaray hopes to affirm a "new" subject that is fluid, multiple, changing and temporal.

In so doing, however, all of the Nietzschean metaphysics remains intact, and her understanding of this new subjectivity does not radically alter from the Cartesian ground that was operative for Nietzsche.[94] Nietzsche can partly be seen as a precursor to the modification of the Cartesian subject that occurred in psycho-analysis by insisting on the unconscious workings in the fictive projections of the self in will to power. For Irigaray, however, it is Lacan's rereading of Freud that provides the basic understanding of her view of subjectivity, even though she reads Lacan as being trapped within a phallogocentric understanding that is based on a logic of solidity.[95] Nevertheless, Irigaray accepts the fundamental principles involved in Lacan's theory of the construction and posit-ing of the (sexed) subject.

But has Lacanian psychoanalysis divorced itself completely from a Cartesian understanding of the subject? The structuration of the subject in Lacan is subject to the order of the Other, that is, the unconscious that has always already been marked by the phallus. For Lacan, the unconscious is, however, structured like a language. The subject comes to be in language, where it slips away under the succession of signifiers. Suspended from signification, the subject is subject to the unconscious. This means that it is not a living substance, it is not a substance in the metaphysical sense of the word, it is not a being of knowledge, nor is it a *logos* incarnate. For Lacan, the "I" is the Cartesian subject which appears temporally when doubt is recognized as certitude of the thinking "I". The subject is thus ex-centrically centered and agitated by the Other through slips of the tongue, jokes, dreams, – in short, the excessive workings of the signifier that has freed itself from the signified.

Lacan draws rigorous consequences from this. First, if the exercise of language constitutes the foundation of subjectivity, then the "I" is a moment in discourse. The speaking subject is thus sustained by the chain of signification. Second, since Lacan remains within a notion of the sign and of signification, the "I" represents something for someone. The signifier represents a subject for another signifier. Therefore, its ground is in language.

In this logic, the subject is born in so far as in the field of the Other, the signifier emerges. However, like Narcissus, it is victim to temporality and to death, and as such, it is nothing.

If in the Lacanian psychoanalytic understanding of the subject, its unity and self-sameness is undermined, it does not follow that the Cartesian subject is completely rejected. Instead, what has taken place is that the subject is temporally only partially present and grounded in its self-certitude. Only through the process of *interpretation*, that is, through a hermeneutics of the signifier of the Other, can totality be restored. What is at stake is the method of retrieving this lost memory. The assumption is, however, that psychoanalysis can restore the partial oblivion that is not present to the subject.

It is in this context that we have to approach Irigaray's thinking on the subject in "Speaking of Immemorial Waters". As the return of the repressed, the *mer/mère* can be retrieved and incorporated into a full and different subject, through a critical appropriation of Nietzsche, Lacan (and Heidegger). However, what has been forgotten in the process, is the question of nihilism itself as it permeates in the language where this retrieval is supposed to occur. What happens to Irigaray's project if the new, multiple "I" that will *La dire* is always already subjected to the workings of nihilism and as such is only an epochal symptom of the essential nature of *aletheia* in language – that is, the withdrawal of Being in unconcealment.

CHAPTER II:
Woman's (Un)Truth:
The Dionysian Woman

In *Beyond Good and Evil*,[1] Nietzsche writes on the question of woman and truth and the following quote can be interpreted as analogous to his pronouncement concerning the "raging discordance between art and truth",[2]:

> From the beginning, nothing has been more alien, repugnant, and hostile to woman than truth – her great art is the lie, her highest concern is mere appearance and beauty.[3]

When Irigaray quotes this passage in her opening paragraph of "Veiled Lips", her second chapter of *Marine Lover*, she vehemently disagrees with Nietzsche's fundamental presupposition in making his remark, namely that "nothing has been more alien [...] to woman than truth". To Irigaray the lie, appearance and beauty are not foreign to truth, but are in fact proper to it. It is rather a question of sameness; difference understood as binary oppositions can never speak of difference. It is opposite to, but nevertheless determined by, sameness. What would truly be alien or foreign to truth, would have to be found "elsewhere". However, within Nietzsche's economy of truth, this possibility has been forgotten.

Irigaray's deconstruction of the multiple figurations of woman in Nietzsche reveals his complicity in Western metaphysics. Pointing to Nietzsche's complicity in Platonic mimesis, Irigaray demonstrates how Nietzsche's understanding of woman remains confined within the paradigm of Echo of Narcissus, in which Echo cannot be perceived as other than its double. Echo's function in Ovid's mythical poem is to accompany the movement of Narcissus' self-reflection, to adorn and to deploy his self-representation, while keeping the integrity of the image intact. In this sense, woman's femininity, defined within this narcissistic "echo-nomy", ensures the smooth workings of this mimetic machinery. But woman cannot be reduced to femininity, says Irigaray:

But woman? Is not reduced to mere femininity. Or to false-hood, or appearance or beauty. Short of staying out of it, (idem, p. 232) and projecting at (from) a distance that other of the self to which truth is, from the outset, hostile: falsehood, as well as beauty and appearance, ... Although femaleness has taken it/them as part of her forms, although she cannot do without it/them if she is to pass for what it is: the truth.[4]

Within the philosophic discourse of truth as we know it from Plato onwards, woman has become the incarnation of that which is erroneous, deceitful, but nevertheless beautiful, like Helen of Troy. For Plato, woman's materiality and her sensuousness are the cause of her imperfection, whereas man's self-image, generated within the principle of *eidos*[5] as the idea(l) image of truth, accounts for his perfection.

Conversely, for Nietzsche, woman's beauty exists precisely in her material imperfection and as such exemplifies the superior principle of illusion as opposed to truth. But in Plato as well as in Nietzsche, woman's femininity has always already been appropri-ated as the negative counterpart to the masculine economy of truth. Femininity is consequently a necessary element for this economy to be operational. Woman does not enter into this economy other than as the negative function in a binary opposition, which says nothing at all about her potentiality for being.

In fact, the aphorism in question from *Beyond Good and Evil* seeks to ridicule woman's attempt to "find herself" within the scientific discourse of truth that Nietzsche so much despises. When Nietzsche claims that "nothing is more alien to woman than truth", we have to understand his statement within the context of his own position with regard to truth.

If woman in a Socratic gesture seeks to enlighten herself and others about herself, her gesture becomes equally as futile and nihilistic as that of the pedantic scientist so often ridiculed by Nietzsche. When woman likewise puts on airs of the philosopher, she becomes an easy target for Nietzsche's ironic scrutiny.

Nietzsche's position thus questions woman's ability to actually *desire* enlightenment about herself. Given that for Nietzsche she embodies the simulacrum, the illusion and everything that he views as alien to this kind of reasoning logic, if woman is "true" to her "untrue" self, (which is, of course, a paradox in itself), then she cannot possibly desire to enlighten herself nor anyone else about herself. Irigaray's contention is, however, that the very economy of truth, which in its essence requires the "echo-nomy" of the lie as its opposite, are both forms of sameness. In her assigned function within this mimetic economy, woman has had to assume this identity of un-truth in order for this paradigm to uphold itself. As such, her identity could not do without (*s'en passer*) this lie that she herself is said to embody in order for her to pass herself off as (*passer pour*) the other of the same.

In his stance against Platonism and Christianity, Nietzsche transvalues the Platonic and Christian devaluation of the body and the sensuous and instead welcomes woman as the material embodiment of sensuous being. In either case, Irigaray holds that woman's femininity thus defined says nothing about what woman's being might potentially be, but says everything about the function of femininity within this economy of masculine truth and sameness.

But we keep forgetting, claims Irigaray, that these significations do not speak of woman's (sexual) difference, but are instead results of a philosophical construct that has appropriated her (potential) being into an assigned position within a paradigm that essentially embraces sameness and cannot tolerate (sexual) difference. For Irigaray it matters little that Nietzsche transvalues woman's materiality and thus elevates her alleged affinity with lying (as opposed to truth), appearance (as opposed to Platonic reality) and beauty (as opposed to ugliness) into the principle of will to power as art.

The comic effect that Nietzsche aspires to in his ridiculing of this scientific endeavor on the part of woman, is of course aimed at undermining the foundation for the feminist movement emerging at that time. In the true fashion of most civil rights movements, the feminists sought to legitimize their plight within the parameters of the Enlightenment tradition. Thus, he mockingly refers to the Kantian aspect of their advocacy:

> Woman wants to become self-reliant – and for that reason she is beginning to enlighten men about "woman as such:" this is one of the worst developments of the general *uglification* of Europe. For what must these clumsy attempts of women at scientific self-exposure bring to light![6]

It is interesting to note that Nietzsche in his aforementioned aphorism opposes the noise of these contemporary female voices to that of "holy Aristophanes".[7] While lamenting the fact that women now have taken up this (to him despicable) scientific project that had previously been reserved to "man's lot", woman has become "untrue" to herself, and Nietzsche cannot help but be suspicious of her ability to "write about 'woman'". For him, it is fundamentally contrary to her nature to desire enlightenment about herself, just as it is contrary for art to want to enlighten itself about itself. It is in the light of these considerations that we must interpret the following provocative and ironic statement: "And I think it is a real friend of women that councils them today: *mulier taceat de muliere* [woman should be silent about woman]."[8]

The question then arises: Who should speak about woman? Since Nietzsche himself never seems to shy away from any pronouncements on the question of woman, one must assume that it is completely appropriate that he speaks when he so desires. Likewise, Aristophanes seems to have an equal god-given right and has even acquired the epithet "holy" in light of his treatment of the subject.

It is interesting to note that Nietzsche highlights Aristophanes' contribution, since his play *Lysistrata*[9] has in the most recent past been (perhaps erroneously) appropriated within the feminist struggle. In his comedy, Aristophanes playfully dramatizes how the women of Athens organize a sex-strike in order to stop the war-economy of the city. However, in order for the women to be effective, they have to seize the "phallus", that is, they have to seize the Acropolis as well as to mobilize an army, armed with weapons made of household items. Moreover, Lysistrata, the "most virile of women",[10] assumes the role of the leader of the uprising.

In Aristophanes' account of the "feminine" menace, it is shown that in order for women to act and to speak within this economy, they have to assume a *mimetic* role, which means that they must *mime* the order of the "phallus". Eventually, when everything is said and done, however, the war ends, and the women are victorious, but the order still remains the same. The women return to their prior domestic roles and the men return home as the uncontested leaders and life resumes as previously.

This return to established order is a state of affairs that is always repeated in comedy, and is perhaps intrinsic to the comic gesture as such. In the (happy) ending of comedy, the *polis* always remains intact, while in tragedy, the very foundation of the *polis* is undermined and the hero is irretrievably destroyed.[11] One might therefore question the stance taken by the feminist movement in regards to *Lysistrata*, which has previously been seen as an ancient "feminist" play. In my reading, I would like to emphasize the conservative elements in comedy in general and in *Lysistrata* in particular. If a feminist uprising can only be effected within the masculine economy, and its outcome is the solidification of this order, then does this play truly speak in the interest of feminism? Furthermore, it is difficult to understand why Nietzsche hailed Aristophanes in light of this reading. The only reason that comes to mind is that he revealed the *mimetic* nature of the women's rebellion, and ultimately its futility.

Irigaray speaks to the question of the comic in terms of "the comedy of the other (*la comédie de l'autre*)". To her, the comic belongs to the order of the same as this other aspect that truth does not always appreciate. But in Aristophanes' play, the comic effect is created by the role-reversal, whereby the archaic roles become accentuated and exaggerated and the comic is thus found in the excess and transgression generated by the reversal. Thus, the comic relies on the mimetic stance taken by the woman. But in order for there to be a happy ending, the struggle has to be resolved and the comic must be eliminated.

Irigaray points to the fact that in general, the comic seems to be attributed to the "other" within the masculine economy of truth, that is, to woman. As such it becomes the mask that she is expected to wear in the performance of the play between the sexes; as a repository for that which exceeds truth. As truth's parody and its ridiculousness, woman has become the repository for that which must be expelled from and foreign to truth in order for it to "keep its face". Paradoxically, in Nietzsche's aphorism, woman is both what is ridiculed and what is elevated as the new (un)truth of the lie. The irony that underlies all of the aphorism makes the masking effect of the comic even more ambiguous.

When Irigaray then impertinently transgresses Nietzsche's advice to remain silent about woman, does she escape the mimetic trap into which women have traditionally been forced? Can she possibly overturn the state of affairs that has reigned from Plato to Nietzsche and thus claim to be capable of speaking *differently* about women? Or, does she perhaps attempt to show that no matter how vehemently she speaks/writes, she will always be silent (to men) on the question of woman? If every theory of the subject has always already been appropriated by the masculine, then is it in fact possible for woman to speak? Will she not always have to pass for a masculine subject in order to have a language at all, and then in the process by necessity "lose herself?" Is this what she attempts to allude to in the title of the chapter, "Veiled lips?". If her lips are veiled, does she thereby suggest that women have no language because their language/body has thus been hidden?

A problem arises for Irigaray in the interpretation of the mimetic gestures of the hysterical woman who assures the corporal dissimulation of the comic. As the incarnation of simulation, the hysteric's gestures and grimaces are characteristically mimetic and therefore feigned, yet without feigning. Are women to identify with the contortions and convulsions of the tortured hysterical woman? Isn't her compulsive mimicking of learned gestures of femininity a truly tragic comedy in itself?

But for Nietzsche, woman's mimicking is supposedly a testimony to her status as a work of art. For Irigaray, the performance of the hysteric yields a different story:

> Mastery asserts itself by skirting such naked obscenity. A disgrace to the whole theater of representation. Irreducible

contortion of a nature mimicking the residue of a properly staged mimicry. Why do women, our women, lie so poorly?[12]

According to Irigaray, the hysteric's explicit sexual gestures reveal an obscenity that becomes horrific, precisely because the veils of repression are absent. In Freud's account of the hysteric, he proposes the following hypothesis, which seems to support Irigaray's interpretation of the signification of her gestures:

> If it be true that the causes of the hysterical disorders are to be found in the intimacies of the patient's psycho-sexual life, and that the hysterical symptoms are the expression of their most secret and repressed wishes, then the complete exposition of a case of hysteria is bound to involve the revelation of those intimacies and the betrayal of those secrets.[13]

The revelation of those intimacies and secrets which are spoken in the hysteric's contorted movements and in her silence, becomes for Irigaray a dionysian spectacle in which the horrible appears. But Irigaray does not understand this destructive theater in terms of the Nietzschean duality between the Dionysian and the Apollonian described in *The Birth of Tragedy*.[14]

For Nietzsche, the Attic tragedy finds its sublime expression in the fusion between the two forces generated from the gods Dionysus and Apollo. The Dionysian finds expression in the choral lyric as the spirit of music that provides the primordial link with the spirit of nature in all of its horrific splendor and which has the power to fragment the unity of the Apollonian force of individuation created by the power of illusion that creates the image of the spectacle.

Thus, when the noble image of Oedipus as the tragic hero in Sophocles' *Oedipus the King*[15] gradually disintegrated under the forces of necessity (*ananke*), what emerges is the raw destructive power of nature which has the power to annihilate the ground of the *polis* on which the tragic hero rests. The Dionysian wisdom, which Oedipus in his blindness finally sees, is for Nietzsche an abominable event:

Indeed, the myth seems to wish to whisper to us that wisdom, and particularly Dionysian wisdom, is an unnatural abomination; that he who by means of his knowledge plunges nature into the abyss of destruction must also suffer the dissolution of nature in his own person.[16]

Irigaray's interpretation of the Dionysian spectacle of the hysteric does not, however, operate within the Nietzschean duality of individuation and disintegration, but claims that this *dionysiaque* indicates instead a "surplus from before (*surplus d'avant*)", prior to any knowledge of unity, wholeness or individuation. The hysteric's primordial fragmentation must therefore not be understood within the Nietzschean Dionysian/Apollonian duality that presupposes an established unity that is subsequently disintegrated. Rather, the fragmentation must instead be read as a primordial surplus "always-already-there". In this sense the hysteric exemplifies for Irigaray a primordial multiple fragmentation from which (an illusory) unity might subsequently emerge.

Nietzsche/Freud relegate to the hysteric the function of the "other" as the prototype of woman *par excellence* in an effort to traverse the lack of veils in a horrific (feminine) nature. As a depository for the fantasm of the other (of the same), the hysteric comes to represent a mimetic veil that is attributed to her in an effort to dispose of/deposit into her, the other of the same. In other terms, she comes to signify that which is truly "other", that is, woman as the simulacrum, at the same time as she functions as the "truth" of woman as illusory artifact. In either case, death permeates her artificial gestures and seems to be operationalized in the figure of the hysteric/woman, whether the desire is for pleasure or for pain.

In Nietzsche's stance against Platonism and Christianity and their common pursuit of the "true world" obtainable through the virtuous endeavor of the sage and the pious man, he posits in his *Twilight of the Idols*:

(Progress of the idea: it becomes more subtle, insidious, incomprehensible – *it becomes female*, it becomes Christian.)[17]

Nietzsche indicates with this pronouncement[18] that if the error becomes the "truth" of pleasure, then the "idea" becomes woman. He thus aligns error, woman, and the Christian. What takes place in the Nietzschean transposition of the "idea" of woman, is predominantly merely a change from one realm of representation to another. In the Platonic scheme, the "eternal feminine" must be devalued because of her primordial connection with temporal and sensuous, nature. With Nietzsche, the representation changes to a possibility "of a different idea" as a new resource of a(n artistic) force, with remnants from the memory of Dionysus. It is in this sense that Irigaray reads his juxtaposition of woman with the Christian.

Nietzsche identifies a progress as having taken place in the "History of an Error", which might be read as synonymous with the "History of Western Metaphysics". With the advent of nihilism, subjectivity becomes perspectival, and truth becomes by implication void of universal validity. The idea is transformed from eternal truth to "woman", now understood as the affirmation of will to power as art in all of its fictive splendor. In *Spurs*, Derrida speaks of the movement to which woman has been subjected throughout the history of Western metaphysics and points to the third and final position of woman that Nietzsche hails in the above mentioned quote:

> In the instance of the third proposition, however, beyond the double negation of the first two, woman is recognized and affirmed as an affirmative power, a dissimulatress, an artist, a dionysiac. And no longer is it man who affirms her. She affirms herself, in and of herself, in man.[19]

However, the fact that Nietzsche puts the entire quote from *The Twilight of the Idols* in parenthesis, a gesture which marks distance, signifies for Irigaray Nietzsche's attempts to cloister *le féminin* in a renewed display of the idea. Nietzsche further elaborates on the importance of distance in another meditation on the question in *The Gay Science*:

> The magic and the most powerful effect of women, is, in philo-

sophical language, action at a distance, *actio in distans*; but this requires first of all and above all – *distance*.[20]

But even Nietzsche's new dressed-up version of the idea as woman remains too coldly theoretical. And, in its resemblance to "being", it seems to have become devoid of all sensuality. One might in fact say that Nietzsche has performed a biting critique of the history of metaphysics in the figure of the vampire, but in the process of transvaluation, he manages to suck the blood out of his newfound "idea". Irigaray chooses the following words to describe the unfortunate bloodletting of woman that has taken place:

Something red was lacking, a hint of blood and guts to revive the will, and restore its strength. A wound. Which however will only be opened up in its representation from within that extra setting: the brackets.[21]

However, Nietzsche's quote has been elevated from an aphorism consisting of six points, all spelled out in numerical order from one to six. Nietzsche structures his aphorism in such a way that under each point he affirms a proposition which is then followed by another one in parenthesis. Thus, each point contains two propositions, the last of which occurs in parenthesis. Under point number two, the following proposition precedes the one in parenthesis quoted by Irigaray:

2. The true world – unattainable for now, but promised for the sage, the pious, the virtuous man ("for the sinner who repents").[22]

In the light of the Platonic scheme which has hitherto dominated philosophy, the "true" world could only be attained in the transcendent world of the "idea" thought as eternally true. Nietzsche ironically posits the advent of woman (in the image of the "eternal feminine") and the Christian (in the image of the pious man) as progress when these become fetishized images of the idea. He argues that we must eventually do away with the notion of the "true world" altogether, something that he proclaims under point six in the same aphorism:

6. The true world – we have abolished. What world has remained? The apparent one perhaps? But no! *With the true world we have also abolished the apparent one.*

(Noon; moment of the briefest shadow; end of the longest error; high point of humanity; INCIPIT ZARATHOUSTRA.)[23]

The first thing that I would like to point out in regard to Irigaray's interpretation of the quote, is that the parenthesis is not exclusively used in his postulate pertaining to the statement that the idea becomes woman; it is a stylistic device used throughout the entire aphorism, and its significance(s) should therefore be considered in relation to the whole aphorism. Second, the parenthesis does not necessarily and exclusively connote distance and containment (of *le féminin*), which Irigaray chooses to emphasize. If meaning is always multiple and in flux, then does not Irigaray herself violate the principle of polysemy in her reading of Nietzsche's enframing parenthesis?

For Irigaray, the encirclement of woman performed by the parenthesis symptomatically comes to stand for the movement of sign-ification of the sign *per se*. She sees the double veiling that takes place of woman in Nietzsche's aphorism as the sur-plus of ideas that, doubly enveloped, releases from its reserve the making or doing **as** the sign:

The articulation of two repetitions, of two different circles around the re-beginning, isn't this always, and still, the way a sign is made? And is "woman" – plus femininity – anything but that residue of ideas that, once it has been doubly wrapped up, serves to capture doing as sign?[24]

The woman *as* sign in this respect exemplifies the *lack* or absence inherent in the re-presentation and as such she gives herself to be that which she is not, – an operation which is always at work in the game of the "other". Irigaray links this lack to the psychoanalytic theory of castration theorized both by Freud and Lacan whereby the question of the (re)presentation of woman moves from the possibility of present-ing herself (*se donner*) to that of giving itself *as* (*se donner pour*) something. Or else woman operates in an undecidable between truth and appearances, as in the Nietzschean schema. But in all cases, the femininity of woman will still remain the "other" of the same. Even when woman is elevated into a "new truth" the operation of castration remains intact.

With Nietzsche, art has the capacity to gather everything, even thinking. But it will always appear *as* something, which appears under the sway of Apollonian illusion. In this context, Irigaray poses the following questions:

> Castration?[25] Wasn't that, precisely, the gesture of repetition which gave the key to the whole stage set by the same? And therefore gave it some play, gave the game the possibility: to be played. In the second or third degree: the Apollonian dream, the Socratic truth, the simulacrum, (both of them within a certain indifference, a repeat that suspends the gash between them, covers the [female] one and the other and yet never really does so, still adhering to a belief in difference – if only to play with it).[26]

For Irigaray, castration is but a simulacrum, whose main function is to set the operation into *play*, even if it has lost its power of differentiation:

> Castration would merely be some simulacrum – with nothing added on – unless the other had nothing, and is not lent what she doesn't have, what she would have been allowed only to take care of. So that she can threaten, by playing or not playing according to the charge she has been invested with – of castration. Castration might be interpreted as a simulacrum used to frighten oneself, and therefore as a source of pleasure in continuing the game.[27]

It is thus in the order of the sign that woman is subject to castration and has to become the depository for absence, death and lack. As such, woman as sign constitutes the "other" which the masculine subject fears above all, since it robs him of his possibility of mastery.

However, with the advent of Nietzsche, the *illusion* inherent in signification can finally be acknowledged, which he does through his philosophy of nihilism with the phrase "God is dead". The simulation necessary for the play of signs to unfold embraces the (simulated) castration that has taken place in relation to philosophy's power to speak totality. But Irigaray asks if this move, instead of undermining the position of mastery sought by the Socratic subject, does not in fact solidify the (illusion of) mastery by incorporating everything within its artistic play of the subjective will, thus reducing it all to a play of *sameness*:

Perhaps by admitting the part played by illusion, by claiming it openly, airing it publicly, one is cleared of the burden of a secret, the guilt of concealment, of the pure and simple assurance of being adequate to mastery. Not by losing. Especially if the scenario is now presumed to be *general*. Including this residue: the other would threaten castration. The other? Of the same? If castration means the same thing as: kill him, if it is equivalent to death, then the other is equivalent to the same. Or else perpetuates the alternation of everything and nothing. Fulfilling the master's desire. Which he can dress up differently, according to the historical moment.[28]

Generally, woman gives herself *for* (something or someone). Her only being within this representational theatre is *as* this nothing that resists representation. As castrated, woman becomes the absolute spot in the economy of signs or the absurd in the comedy of the other. Irigaray chooses to characterize this (non)position of woman in the following terms:

Castrating is the "absolute" spot in the economy of signs. The absurd: which is not sublated, nor repeated in any way at all. Neither event, nor phenomenon, nor form, nor ideality ... That which cannot be represented.[29]

Concealed within the economy of the same, woman is presented *as* something that she is not, namely femininity, which means that she is a castrated man. Simply put, how can she possibly be castrated when she never in fact had a penis? Thus, she can only give herself *as* this negative of man. What woman is, can only emerge as a *nothing* at the heart of the economy that has attempted to contain her being within its own sameness.

But for Irigaray, woman cannot be spoken in any of the denominations hitherto given to her:

> The/a woman is not to be reabsorbed into truth, or appearance, or semblances. Provided that she still manages to withold herself from the generalization of the stage set.[30]

Woman only enters into this (masculine) signification *as* the object, the stake, the repetition of a negation or as de-negation. She has to lend herself to this position of exclusion thought either as repression, or, as outside of representation altogether. If she appears at all, it is only to thereby lose herself.

This symbolic murder of woman through the category of femininity has found expression in a host of roles in the course of the last centuries, Irigaray says:

> Since several centuries of silence have taken on quite a number of roles: echo, place, interval, abyss, thing, possibility of repetition, or articulation ... mirror ...[31]

However, this *nothing* which then has become the ground upon which the masculine edifice has been erected, whether we think of it in terms of the unconscious, which Irigaray contends women do not have, but **are,**[32] or as the silent primordial ground that is essentially undecidable, nevertheless signals an outside, an in-itself or an elsewhere, outside of the enframing view of that which has hitherto been thought.

ii

The major thrust of Irigaray's writing attempts to make a bridge to this "elsewhere", which she nominates *le féminin*. *Le féminin* differs from femininity in that it does not enter into the economy of mimesis other than as that which defies representation, as absence or as silence, but it comes into play only within an economy that is *specific* to itself, and thus attains its value from its different form(s).

In *Ce sexe qui n'en est pas un*, Irigaray explores this morphologic of difference which she claims to have discovered in the very form(s) of the female sexual organs. In its/their morphology, it/they defy the traditional notions of unity, sameness and solidity and speak instead to the principle of multiplicity, difference and fluidity. Characteristically, she describes the connection between the form(s) of the feminine sex and the traditional paradigm of thought in the following way:

> If the female sex takes place by embracing itself, by endlessly sharing and exchanging its lips, its edges, its borders, and their "content", as it ceaselessly becomes other, no stability of essence is proper to her. She has a place in the openness of a relation to the other whom she does not take into herself, like a whore, but to whom she continuously gives birth.[33]

In the above, it is not a question of giving birth in the empirical sense of the word. Woman is therefore not derived from the mother, except if one wants to give a term for her growth and to her gift of life. The mother is a woman according to a certain mode of accomplishment of this operation, that is, of giving life. But the/a woman can already sub-sist to be double in herself, that is, both the one and the other. In this way she continuously exchanges herself in the other, without ever being *proper* to herself or to the other. Thus, *le féminin* is totally foreign to the possibility of unity, of possession in the sense of belonging (to someone/thing), even reflexively, as belonging to herself.

At this juncture, Irigaray makes the startling pronouncement:

> The feminine goes beyond "phenomenology". Were it not for the demands of the economy of sameness. Because "she" affects herself already (within herself) without the appearance of a sensible sign. She has no overriding need to produce herself under any form whatever.[34]

What emerges here is an indirect critique of phenomenology and its proclaimed philosophy of beings, including the subject itself. With this pronouncement, Irigaray thus separates her thinking from traditional phenomenologists, and even perhaps by implication, Heidegger.

If we are to understand her in the sense that all beings that emerge within the phenomenological objective are always already contaminated with the "echo-nomy of (phallic) truth" as it emerges from Plato and Aristotle onwards, then *le féminin* must be understood to reside outside the realm of these confines.

But *le féminin* does not have to appear at all, and must therefore not be confined to the erquirements of a (coherent, solid, unified) phenomenological form in order to be. Her being might consequently be found in her lack of being, and this default of being might actually also reside in her excess (*en plus*). What most clearly seems to be the target here is the Cartesian and later phenomenological obsession with certainty, first of the subject and subsequently of the object that the subject understands/perceives.

Another question to Irigaray would be: If *le féminin* resides outside the phenomenological framework and perhaps outside the confines of the hermeneutic circle, then how does Irigaray have access to this "elsewhere?" What grants her power to reach inside this domain and to (poetically) speak (its being), if in fact it has no being?[35] By the same token, how can it possibly be anything – multiple, fluid, without limits, without property and free-flowing pleasure – if it in fact has no being? And, what is the status of Irigaray's language when she makes these pronouncements? Finally, how does the question of nihilism enter into this problematic?

Irigaray claims that *le féminin* defies the very possibility of identity and that the profundity which woman contains, is one that sub-sists under the general "echo-nomy" of truth. Since *le féminin* never can be monolithic, she will always encompass multiplicity within herself(ves). *Le féminin* exists prior to and is more primordial than the systems of thought that have hitherto attempted to contain woman, whether that be "truth" or "error", which both belong to the logic of the *same*.

But *le féminin*'s functioning within itself remains ludic, in the most open-ended sense of that which is free and playful. She refers to the workings of *le hasard* in the determination of what woman will be. But she will always give herself *as* something, in her words: "Chance – the deal/deals her. Can only be dealt out for what he/she is not."[36]

This seemingly simple statement contains rather far-reaching implications if we interpret it to mean that chance determines how woman is given, and she will appear only in terms of what "he"/"she" is not. What this seems to suggest is that woman is forever subjected to the phenomenological apparatus foreign to her, but belonging to man, who will always attempt to appropriate her within his phenomenological forms which will in turn negate and deny her existence. Therefore, she can only "give herself for/as" something that she is not.

Irigaray's statement seems on the one hand to follow in the Heideggerian path in her acknowledgement of the receptive role given to woman in regard to her possibility for being, and she seems to adhere to the Heideggerian notion of the *as-structure* in her laying out of the problem connected to how woman must "*se donner pour*" something that is essentially foreign to her in order for her to appear at all within the dominant discourse. On the other hand, she defies the necessity of appropriation in her theorizing on *le féminin* and seems thereby to fly in the face of Heidegger's notion of *Ereignis*.

First, in Heidegger's *Being and Time*, he defines phenomenon "in the phenomenological sense as that which shows itself as Being as and as a structure of Being".[37] Thus, in an attempt to give a phenomenological description of the world, he exhibits the Being of those entities that he perceives as present-at-hand within the world, and then fixes them within concepts that to him are categorical.

Irigaray's objections to this endeavor would, of course, be manifold. In what she perceives to be his privileging of sight in his pursuit of the phenomenon, Heidegger would of course be implicated in Platonic mimesis as its oculocentrism. Furthermore, Irigaray would then point to Heidegger's dependance on what she would call the "echo-nomy" of truth in his attempt to frame the phenomenon within the categorical and the conceptual.

On this basis, Irigaray rejects phenomenology as a valid structure through which *le féminin* could be approached. Because *le féminin* would yield nothing to be shown within the phenomenological optics, and since it can only see what it has already seen, it cannot possibly do justice to *le féminin*'s potentiality for Being.

However, Heidegger's thinking on the question of temporality as it pertains to the question of Being remains one of the most important contributions to 20th century thinking, and Irigaray is of course no stranger to his work. In my previous treatment of the *as-structure*, I pointed to Heidegger's emphasis of the (ontological) difference that exists between the existential-hermeneutical "as" through which Dasein circumspectively understands itself within a totality of involvements and the apophantical "as" of the assertion that is always derivative of the prior. In Western metaphysics from Aristotle onwards, Heidegger claims there has been a forgetfulness of this primordial understanding provided in the existential-hermeneutical "as" and simultaneously a privileging of the apophantical "as" which obeys the ontical logic of the theoretical interpretation.

It seems to me that Irigaray accepts Heidegger's observation that the kind of interpretation that understands the world apophantically cannot pay heed to the Being question. What it forgets is that something is hidden from view in this appropriation of the present-at-hand. Therefore, one might say that Irigaray uses a Heideggerian path of thinking in her exploration of *le féminin* in the sense that she reveals how it cannot appear as other than as "femininity", which shows itself as the negative double of the logical categories that already exist, that is, in a sameness to that which is privileged, namely the masculine, unity, solidity and sameness.

Even though woman within this "as"-structure has to conform to this paradigm as a negation of the same, she has still been appropriated as a negative but indifferent counterpart. Thus, caught within the "as"-structure of the already existing theoretical paradigms, chance, which rules the destiny of this history of being as it has unfolded itself, has relegated woman to giving herself out to be the same of the same.

When Nietzsche furthermore thinks woman as the error of

metaphysics, as that which ironically appears as something different than what it is, *ce qu'elle n'est pas*, he then posits woman as
becoming and as perpetual change. But for Irigaray, Nietzsche's
positioning of woman as a counterpart to the Platonic scheme of
truth, that is, as erring from the Platonic time of essence, permanence and self-identity, cannot possibly let woman's *difference*
emerge since he remains firmly lodged within this Platonic duality
of truth/error, permanence/change, and self-identity/non-identity.
Thus, woman's profundity has been alternately denigrated or valor-
ized within this duality, and Nietzsche's contribution does not
radically diverge from that of his previous fellow philosophers.
According to different moments in history, "woman" has emerged
both as truth and as error, or even as both, but *le féminin* has yet to
emerge in its *difference*.

This observation made by Irigaray opens up the following
questions, only indirectly approached by Irigaray. It brings to the
fore the problem of the *as*-structure as Heidegger thought it in its
relationship to nihilism, defined as synonymous with the "history
of Being". Irigaray approaches the question of nihilism in terms of
the valorization and devaluation of "woman" as she has figured in
Western metaphysics, and as such she problematizes both
Nietzsche's and Heidegger's thinking on the nihilism question.

Nietzsche defined nihilism in the terms of the fact "that the
highest values devaluate themselves". "Woman" has attained the
status of value within metaphysical thinking and as such "she" had
been subject to subsequent devaluation before Nietzsche came
along to "save" woman through his transvaluation. Heidegger, on
the other hand, understands nihilism as the history of Western
metaphysics and therefore as the history of Being, and has pointed
out how the two are inextricably linked. Through his valuative
philosophy, Nietzsche reverses Platonism in the sense that that
which was previously devalued is now valued. As a transvalued
value, "woman" is implicated in this operation, since she seems to
figure at the center of the nihilism problematic.

Irigaray's treatment of the possible profundity of woman as it is
thought by metaphysics in general and by Nietzsche in particular
seems to resonate in Heidegger's thinking in his "Nihilism as
Determined by the History of Being".[38] In an attempt to assess

Nietzsche's position in relation to the metaphysical tradition and his alleged overcoming of nihilism through his valuative will to power, Heidegger points to the inability of Nietzsche to think the Being question.

Like most of his predecessors, Nietzsche remains trapped within metaphysics, but fails to see that metaphysics reaches deeper than metaphysics itself. That to which it reaches belongs to a different realm, and appears only as an enigma:

> According to its essence, nihilism is the history of the promise, in which Being itself saves itself in a mystery which is itself historical and which preserves the unconcealment of Being from that history in the form of metaphysics. The whole of the essence of nihilism, to the extent that – as the history of Being – it bestows itself as an abode for the essence of man, grants thinking everything that is to be thought. Consequently, what is given to thinking as to be thought we call *the enigma*.[39]

For Heidegger, Being is what gives rise to thought, it "gives food for thought", and "Being, the promise of the unconcealment as the history of the secret, is itself the enigma".[40] It is therefore Being itself that gives rise to metaphysics, and it follows that metaphysics cannot possibly determine the enigma of Being. In Heidegger's view, "the unworthy game of hide and seek which is supposed to be played between the irrational and the rational is exposed in all its mindlessness".[41]

The implication of this is, for Heidegger, that the essence of nihilism in the history of Being is not something that can be produced in thought. Rather, that which is given "reality" in metaphysics can only be on the basis of the essential history of Being itself which allows beings to be through the default of Being. Heidegger concludes by saying that "[t]he essence of nihilism in the history of Being takes place as the history of the secret".[42]

Irigaray seems on the one hand to rely on Heidegger's thinking in her attempt to question Nietzsche's reversed valuation of woman as becoming, as error or as illusion when she ironically echoes Heidegger by positing: "Full awareness – dissimulation that hides (itself)/(*la pleine connaissance – la dissimulation qui (se) dérobe*).[43] But in the following, she seems to respond to the above assertion made by Heidegger when she claims that woman's profundity cannot be contained in the having knowledge of a secret:

> The depth of a woman cannot be closed up over having – knowledge of a secret. Except from the point of view of the truth in which she is played as a store (of) dissimulation: her representation therein will never have been anything but pretense, in a different way. She is denigrated or valued according to the historical moment. And – both at the same time.[44]

We have previously determined that there was an attempted alignment between "woman" and "Being" in Irigaray.[45] Here, on the other hand, it seems that she distances herself from Heidegger as well as from Nietzsche. If woman cannot be understood in terms of the Nietzschean (trans)valuation of her as the untruth of truth, neither can she be thought through the figure of the secret or the enigma:

> The thing that the depth of woman is supposed to be the hiding place and hiding mechanism for is what representation obliterates even from the visible. For "she", also, is visible. But she is not repeated, reproduced, in traditional representation because she is already split "within herself". And the echonomy in being cannot account for this.[46]

What cannot be thought in traditional representations of woman is that she is always already split, double, or fragmented "within herself (*en elle-même*)". But this splitting seems to take place on a phenomenological – and by implication on an ontical level, exemplified in the figure of "this sex which is not one". In this sense, the "being" of "woman" exceeds the boundaries of the unified phenomenon as it is understood in traditional phenomenological terms.

On the other hand, *le féminin* seems to speak of an ontological difference between that which emerges and that which *le féminin is* in its *difference*, that is, in its absence. If the logic of analogy be at all operative at this level, one might contend that Irigaray has appropriated Heidegger's radical phenomenology in her projection of *le féminin*. As that which in its absence is always already split, and which only appears *as* that which it is not, *le féminin* may be said to speak of an ontological difference akin to Heidegger's differentiation between Being and beings.[47]

Another problem that emerges in this context, is the possible meaning(s) of "within herself". We have to assume that we are not talking about a Kantian notion of an "in itself", which even the most stringent phenomenology declares unattainable.[48] What seems to be at stake is an attempted envisioning of an immediacy that is not implicated in traditional representations determined by unity, self-sameness and identity. Instead, what Irigaray attempts to project is rather *different* "being(s)":

> So, when she touches herself (again), who is "she"? And "herself"? Inseparable, "she" and "herself" are part the one of the other, endlessly. They cannot really be distinguished, though they are not for all that the female same, nor the male same. That can be reassembled within some whole. This is to say again, or further, that it would be impossible to decide definitively which "of the two" would be "she" and which "herself".[49]

For Irigaray, this means that discursively, the subject is not identifiable in its relationship to the object. The "herself (*se*)" cannot be read reflexively, since there is no true property of the self nor is there any identity to "her (*elle*)". In this sense, they exist outside the masculine discourse founded upon the self-identity of the subject and its predicate. In the case of *le féminin*, Irigaray projects a new algebra:

> x is (to, in, ...) y – which still allows passivity to have a place in auto-affection, or else a suspension between activity and passivity in the attribution of being – it will never be known who/what is y in the female.[50]

Undecidability will thus replace certitude and calculability in the "there" of *le féminin*. *Elle* does not possess the instrument that would give her access to her own property, nor to that of the "other". In her function as "other" to the masculine economy, the/a woman remains outside of its objective.

But from this position of outsider, she nevertheless supports its economy. For instance, within the psychoanalytic framework, woman figures as castrated, yet she functions as a fear of castration. But what is important to understand in this mechanism, is that she can uphold the logic of predication without there being anything proper to her in this function. To foresee this would in effect mean the death of the subject whereby the ground is taken away from the solidity of the subject's foundation, and the collage of the forms will subsequently crumble. The horror of the abysmal (wounded) woman would appear, and loss of identity would follow, a loss that can only signify death. Woman thus lives in death, and as the vampire that she is, she causes the subject to become anaemic.

But her function as death does not exhaust her being. There is always that which exceeds death. Woman does not die from death, other than as a subject. In fact, she remains unmarked by this functioning in her sub-sistence underlying all discursivity, which for Irigaray gives her an ontological status as *matière première*:

> Out of the storehouse of matter all forms are born. She brings them into the world, she "produces". From between her lips comes every new figure: a warm glowing heat comes out of that self-embrace and becomes "visible". But once, one single time, and one instant only: beauty. Afterward, or, by default and repetition, there are veils. Unless there be a divine reality.[51]

This status of *matière première* and the "visible" hearkens back to Heidegger's understanding of Being in its relationship to beings. Heidegger says in *Identity and Difference*:

> We speak of the *difference* between Being and beings. The step back goes from what is unthought, from the difference as such, into what gives us thought. That is the *oblivion* of the difference. The oblivion here to be thought is the veiling of the difference as such, thought in terms of concealment; this veiling

has in turn withdrawn itself from the beginning. The oblivion belongs to the difference because the difference belongs to the oblivion. The oblivion does not happen to the difference only afterwards, in consequence of the forgetfulness of human thinking.[52]

Both Irigaray and Heidegger emphasize the ontological difference between Being and beings, or, in Irigaray's terminology, between "first matter (*matière première*)" and "forms". The primordial nature of this difference comes to light as that which is prior to all emergent beings, as that which gives rise to them. Irigaray's discourse pays heed to the figure of the mater-ial aspects of giving birth, whereas in Heidegger's language, emphasis is put on the "giving" as present-ing in language. Both, however, insist on the *difference* inherent between this gift-giving and what is given as well as the oblivion that enshrouds it. *Le féminin* is for Irigaray this oblivion of the difference that cannot be thought in Western metaphysics. Heidegger puts it in the following words:

> The difference between Being and beings is the area within which metaphysics, Western thinking in its entire nature, can be what it is. The step back thus moves out of metaphysics into the essential nature of metaphysics. [...] [D]iscourse about Being and beings can never be pinned down to *one* epoch in the history of the clearing of "Being". Nor does discourse about "Being" ever understand this name in the sense of a genus, an empty generality under which the historically represented doctrines are being subsumed as individual cases. "Being" ever and always speaks as destiny, and thus permeated by tradition.[53]

Like *le féminin*, Heidegger's Being can never assume any identity, but in its unfolding in the clearing of history, it will always be appropriated by tradition and thus always appear as beings, *different* from Being. The "*as*-which" that appears belongs to and is determined by tradition and its destiny is claimed in the event of appropriation [*Ereignis*]. Likewise, *le féminin* will never appear in discourse as that which it is, but always *as* that to which tradition, in its event of appropriation, subjects it; therefore, it has appeared as truth, abyss, death, untruth, art, interval, excess etc. Tradition in this sense determines the destiny of every being. This is where the question of temporality enters the scene. In this context, it seems appropriate to mention Heidegger's pivotal contribution to this problem in his highly influential works *Being and Time* and *On Time and Being*. Throughout his oeuvre, Heidegger has attempted to think this question as it emerges in the metaphysical tradition. In *On Time and Being*, Heidegger writes:

> What is in time and is thus determined by time, we call the temporal. [...] Time and the temporal mean what is perishable, what passes away in the course of time. [...] Being and time determine each other reciprocally, but in such a manner that neither can the former – Being – be addressed as something temporal nor can the latter – time – be addressed as a being.[54]

Irigaray understands beauty as that unique moment at which the form is given birth. However, with the event of appropriation, the form passes into temporality. Simultaneously, the veiling, the doubling occurs as a moment of violence, whereby the *lèvres* that gave birth to these forms are being violated in the shrouding oblivion of this originary birthplace.

By quoting Nietzsche's aphorism # 339 in its entirety, Irigaray reveals how Nietzsche's view of *vita femina* remains clouded by the veiling that hides woman from his view. In his celebration of beauty in the form of the woman, Nietzsche claims the most powerful magic of life to be "covered by a veil interwoven with gold, a veil of beautiful possibilities, sparkling with promise, resistance, bashfulness, mockery, pity, and seduction. Yes, life is a woman".[55] Nietzsche here refers to the Greeks and their prayer to the gods: "Everything beautiful twice and even three times."[56] In her reading, Irigaray shows how Nietzsche fails to understand that it is the repetition that weaves the veil of gold that covers beauty and thus prevents it from reemerging.

For Irigaray, beauty can only emerge once. It is in the doubling and the repetition that beauty is violated, because, what is released in time passes away and cannot possibly be recalled. This letting-be in the opening is something that Western metaphysics cannot tolerate in its attempt to master its beings. Contrary to this desire to fix and master beauty into controllable representations, infinitely repeatable, Irigaray projects her vision of this *different* production:

> Sub-sists the death-life that does not reach, or renounces? individuation in order to keep hold of the self-embrace, nearness, simultaneity... She remains, close, but foreign to mastery, to any form of sublation into the ever threatening representation. Buried in the deepest "depths", primitively, in the swamps of oblivion.[57]

Already with the Greeks, in their two-fold division between mortals and gods, there occurred a privileging of the Apollonian mask of individuation with the ensuing devaluation of the destructive voluptuousness of the Dionysian force. But in Irigaray's view, the birth of both of the gods occults the anterior past of a form-figure from whence they sprung forth, and that is always singular:

> that is apparent, and still tangible. She is beautiful and also has that fragility that comes to her as a result of no longer touching everything: from being distinguished as such in the moment when she first makes her appearance. But dead from (this) birth?[58]

This originary "first matter (*matière première*)" that touches the "whole" exists prior to the coming to be of any gods or mortals. Irigaray refers to it as "earth (*terre*)", the earth that sustains their growth as the figure of the mother that has the power to give life.

Yet, in Western cultures, man's visible (self)erection in his solitary detachment from the mother-earth is threatened by death precisely through this cutting off from his maternal roots. What follows is an oblivion of and a repression of the indebtedness to this "primary mater-ial" through the insistence on an endless repetition of this unique coming to presence in the production of abstract forms, which are eternal because they have no origin.

The justification for the symbolic murder of the "primary matter" and the subsequent valuation of eternal ideal forms is to avoid that which belongs to the sensuous:

[...] pain and pleasure, the violence of the senses, expenditure, a nearness without distinction, ... blood.[59]

Irigaray asks if this valuation of the supra-sensuous alongside the devaluation of the sensuous realm that takes place with the Greeks does not in effect mark the initial refusal and the negation of the "mater-ial" that inaugurates the ethico-political order of patriarchy.

The infancy of patriarchy finds expression, among other figurations, in Greek mythology. Paradoxically, it is to a woman that the necessity of the denial of the mother is attributed. Athena, the goddess of truth and the protectress of the *polis*, exemplifies for Irigaray the appropriation of woman in this patriarchal order. Conceived in the fore-head of Zeus, the God of gods, she inaugurates this order that builds its edifice on the death, denial, and absence of the mother.

Femininity, as it emerges within this *mythos*,[60] becomes a doubling of the law of the Father as God in order to assist him in the totality of his creation. Situated in the middle, between the gods above and men, the gods below, Athena is the mediator, the benevolent do-gooder who acts in the name of neutrality, that is, of justice.

However, this neutrality is only apparent. In truth, her loyalties are always on the side of the father. Irigaray quotes Aeschylus' *Oresteia*,[61] where Athena declares her position as follows:

There is no mother anywhere who gave me birth, and, but for marriage, I am always for the male with all my heart, and strongly on my father's side.[62]

Femininity thus defined functions as an intermediary simulacrum that allows the false to pass for the true, and which effaces the difference *between*. For Irigaray, femininity becomes in Socratic thinking this secret of the production: the absence of the mother and the production of the child solely by the male. Like Athena, Apollo is abhorred by the thought of being likened to his mother's blood-line and he joins in Athena's lamentation on the evils of maternal contamination when he utters:

The mother is no parent of that which is called her child, but only nurse of the new-planted seed that grows. The parent is he who mounts. A stranger she preserves a stranger's seed, if no god interfere. I will show you proof of what I have explained. There can be a father without any mother. There she stands, the living witness, daughter of Olympian Zeus, she who was never fostered in the dark of the womb yet such a child as no goddess could bring to birth.[63]

Between Athena and Apollo there is no difference, they both espouse and speak the law of the father, even if this speech is cleft in an ambiguous *logos* that originates from the oracle. Interestingly, the oracle speaks through a cleft in the earth, but its connection to the earth-mother has been completely silenced. What is heard, is exclusively the words of the father – the sky-god, whose truth is disseminated in the figure and the words of the daughter as well as the son.

What characterizes their speech is sameness. Irigaray claims that this genetic error transposes the scene of truth to the realm of appearance by instituting the (seeming) reign of femininity. Athena comes to represent the circularity of the apparent, into which we have subsequently become trapped:

Reasonable, even speculative, a little warlike: armed to the teeth, but a mediator nevertheless. Between the high and the low, and all the extremes, but with the direction always being projected from the same point. To make a circle, perhaps.[64]

The Socratic system through which this new patriarchal order speaks finds its primary expression and symbolism in the figures of Athena and Apollo. Thus, femininity (and masculinity) becomes disseminated in the thinking of the father. Irretrievably, the mother is lost and woman appears as veiled, devoid of her originary beauty, and unable to touch herself in her wholeness. Her body cloaked, only her face appears, and Athena's lips can only speak a paternal language.

The theme of matricide, on which the patriarchal order rests, figures likewise at the heart of the tragic conflict in the *Oresteia*, where a murder has been committed, namely that of the mother of Orestes, Clytaemestra. In his revenge of the death of his father, Agamemnon, Orestes kills his mother and her new lover, his cousin Aegisthus. Interestingly, it is Apollo who incites Orestes to commit matricide. After the deed has been committed, Orestes is hounded to insanity by the Furies, who are the protectresses of the ancient law of the mother.

In their Dionysian connectedness to the earth and to the ancient spirit of the Fates, the Furies are predominantly invisible, but they express in their paradoxical form the connection between *phusis* and temporality. They are supposedly grotesque midgets who are small like children, but are as ancient as the earth and emit an unbearable stench, since they are in a perpetual process of decomposition. These life-death figures protect the blood-lines and will ensure the vengeance of the mother-murder.

The strife that occurs between the Furies, who in the last play of the trilogy, *The Eumenides*, form the chorus, and the younger gods, Athena and Apollo, is curiously resolved when Athena persuades the Furies to accept her juridical intervention which is decided by the casting of a ballot among the citizens of Athens. As a compensation, she assures them that they have not lost the battle, but that the tribunal solution is just and she promises them in recompense a new dwelling-place:

> In complete honesty I promise you a place of your own, deep hidden under ground that is yours by right, where you shall sit on shining chairs beside the hearth to accept devotions offered by your citizens.[65]

The prime agent behind this solution, is of course Zeus, the god of words, who sees it in his interest to institute the juridical system in the *polis*, whose integrity is assured by the protection of his daughter/mouth-piece Athena. Aeschylus settles this conflict in such a way that justice, under the sway of persuasion, gains ground. The Furies are from now on forever buried and silenced in their deep and subterranean abode.

But what is eliminated with them is the memory of the older order of the mother, from whose blood everything emerges, but who must be forgotten in order for the patriarchal Socratic logic to reign. The tragedy ends with peace, but the price paid for this peaceful situation has been the silencing of the (m)other:

> In the primeval dark of earth-hollows held in high veneration with rights sacrificial bless them, all people, with silence.[66]

Yet another step in the development of the patriarchal order occurs when Socrates subsumes art under the dominance of truth. Socrates derives his form-ideas from Apollo, but his beauty, which previously displayed itself freely in art, now becomes subservient to the "Good". The only way in which the Dionysiac survives, is in the *pathos* of death, which now attains the status of the supreme good. It is in this context that Irigaray interprets Socrates' desire for death, that is, as signifying that he is connected to the dionysian.[67] In this sense, Socrates repays his debt to the primordial mother-nature:

> Those wrenching contradictions that he bore within himself are resolved by his death that pays off the debt knowledge owes to the primitive-mother-nature. The life of Socrates is still a tragedy. But this first and last hero of theory would leave to his posterity only the symbolic repetition of (his) death: the death "for a laugh" of the philosopher whose potion is the *logos*.[68]

But the repercussions of this decisive shift will prove to be detrimental to the figuration of woman in Western metaphysics. With Socrates, the dominance of the forms (*morphe*) over mat(t)er *hule* is already sedimented, and the value of the ex-static teleological pursuit of the "Good/Idea(l)" becomes the ruling principle that equates truth with the will to live a good life. Henceforth, all passions are ordained towards this unique cause, or any excesses that emerge in the pursuit of the "truthful life" are all channelled towards and resolved in divine possession.

The outcome of this ancient strife between matter (*hule*) and form (*morphe*), between Dionysus and Apollo, between the Mother, be it as the *matière première*/Gaia and as Clytaemestra and Zeus and Agamemnon, or between the Furies and the younger gods, constitutes in all its implications a fatal blow to how woman is thought in the Occident.

In *L'oubli de l'air chez Martin Heidegger*, Irigaray elaborates this argument by showing how in the Socratic schema the privileging of *logos* in relation to *phusis* as the emergent, becomes pivotal in this regard:

> La *phusis* est toujours déjà soumise à la technique et à la science: celles du *logos*. Quelque chose de la croissance des étants physiques s'oublie dans la *phusis* du *logos*. Le *phuein* des étants physiques s'oublie dans la métaphysique de l'être. La nature est recrée par le *logos*. Dans l'oubli que ce qui est ainsi refait garde aussi ses qualités physiques. Que l'économie de l'étant physique se rappelle toujours dans toute fabrication de l'homme. Que le corps vivant comme *Gestell* y laisse toujours des traces. Oubliées, elles insistent comme l'impensé et l'impensable du monde que l'homme s'est fabriqué.[69]

Irigaray subsequently questions whether Heidegger does not in fact reduce *phusis* to *techne*, as well as *phuein* to *logos*.[70] She acknowledges that Heidegger has been able to retrace metaphysics towards that which, in the beginning, was lost and remains hidden in it. But according to Irigaray, Heidegger remains trapped in his own privileging of *language*:

> Mais il demeure dans son architechtonique: le *logos*. Cherchant dans l'oubli de celle-ci la cause de la perte, alors que c'est elle qui la détermine. Que la perte et son oubli proviennent d'une *architechne*: du *logos* méta-physique.[71]

Despite these architectonic attempts to enframe woman within the technocratic language of metaphysics, woman remains the "untouchable". Even Heidegger's attempts to retrieve that which has been lost will ultimately fail in Irigaray's view, since he is privileging language as the key to the mystery. *Logos* will in this context have to be understood in the Heideggerian sense of language, and not in the traditional sense of "logic".[72]

But for Irigaray, Heidegger's statement that "language is the house of Being" already attests to the fact that *phusis* can only appear in language and not in its materiality. What is at stake for her, is the resurrection of *phusis* as the memory of the fluid materiality from whence everything emerges, but that cannot be in language such as it has evolved in the West. The resource of this primordial mat(t)er resists the appropriating gesture of *logos* and will never become its property.

It is in this sense that we have to understand the importance imputed to the goddess Athena. As a semblant of woman, her woman-ness remains hidden, and only her paternal face appears. And as the purveyor of truth, Athena exemplifies the seductive power of appearance. Regardless of her preference for the masculine, she refuses marriage and asks of her father to give her eternal virginity. In fact, she is a virile (wo)man "in drag" and as such exemplifies the ambivalence in God's relationship to the mother and to woman:

> Ce qu'on appelera, désormais, la tromperie des femmes. Qui n'est qu'une projection du Père. Parée, la féminité – l'apparaître de la pensée du père sur le pouvoir féminin. S'attributant la puissance maternelle, l'avalant, l'introjectant, il engendre, produit cette fille qui (ne) se donne pour ce qu'elle n'est pas: un simulacre emprunté par le Dieu pour l'assister dans son oeuvre, établir son empire. Du semblant qui prétend se passer de corps, de mort. Le règne de la séduction dans l'apparence – *la vérité*.[73]

Pallas Athena is for Irigaray a (wo)man, veiled with the discourse of the father, and whose persuasion and seduction finds its power in her femininity, which forever separates her from the woman she might have been.

Irigaray quotes Nietzsche's aphorism # 60 in *The Gay Science* to elaborate on this point. Interestingly, this is the same aphorism which Derrida appropriates in the opening of *Éperons*. In this passage Nietzsche is sitting by the sea-shore, musing on the thunderous noise of the surf that Poseidon the earth-shaker makes when he discovers the magic image of a sailboat which glides silently at a distance:

Oh, what ghostly beauty! How magically it touches me! Has all the calm and taciturnity of the world embarked on it? Does my happiness itself sit in this quiet place – my happier ego, my second, departed self? Not to be dead and yet no longer alive? A spiritlike intermediate being: quietly observing, gliding, floating? As the boat that with its white sails moves like an immense butterfly over the dark sea. Yes! To move *over* existence! That's it! That would be something![74]

To Irigaray, when Nietzsche later likens the sailboat to women and believes that his better self is lodged within these quiet dreamlike magical beings that glide past him at a *distance*, he inevitably venerates the deathlike presence of women as "a spiritlike intermediate being". Like the sailboat which seemingly hovers *over* the sea in its veiled distance, so do women for Nietzsche float over existence. In fact, he despises the thought of having to listen to the clattering noise that actually occurs on the sailboat while it sails, as he abhors the thought of having to listen to the petty chatter of women up close.

Only at a distance do they have the effect of deathly beauty, and only as such can they be tolerated. Irigaray interprets this in such a way that Nietzsche cannot stomach women's physical presence nor her natural being. What she might be, in herself and for herself, has to be silenced. Thus, the task of the philosopher becomes to enforce this separation to create a distance, which for him is a prerequisite for beauty to emerge. But for Irigaray, this means to violate, to steal and to veil that which her nature might allow woman to be:

By nature, (a) woman would seem to be at least double. Her "operation" would be to double. But, naturally, the him/her that is nearest. The him/her that is so near that the figure, the shape, even when visible, are blurred in the immediacy of this "act". With no discrimination of model or reproduction. With no interval that can be framed between the one and the other. Infinite growth, ironic proliferation of the natural, that it was perhaps necessary to limit for fear it would ruin mastery. As it sank beneath an ever more.[75]

In her fertile coming and going and in the incessant interlacing of her multiple forms which thwart any opposition between a here and a there, woman remains forever in the open. This proximity, claims Irigaray, is what threatens man's desire for mastery, and consequently, he has always attempted to separate her proliferation by penetrating it with a pointed object, be it with a stiletto, a dagger, a pen, or even an umbrella or a sail.[76] But in his attempt to pry open and create borders and demarcations between that which is naturally open-ended and close-knit, man will, according to Irigaray, only discover the *"fantômes"* that he himself has created in the interval – dreams of life and death. Thus, what is cut off from her in this suture, is nothing that she could possibly lose, because it never belonged to her in the first place.

Nietzsche furthermore emphasizes his dread for woman's nature in the preceding aphorism # 59, where he states:

When we love a woman, we easily conceive a hatred for the nature on account of all of the repulsive natural functions to which every woman is subject. We prefer not to think of all this; but when our soul touches on these matters for once, it shrugs as it were and looks contemptuously at nature: we feel insulted; nature seems to encroach on our possessions, and with the profanest hand at that.[77]

Instead of confronting this horrific nature, Nietzsche prefers to think about soul and form. What he recommends, is for the artist to ignore nature by dreaming and fantasizing.

In this way, the "somnambulists of the day" can rejoice in loving and hating and desiring – woman, without ever having to confront her nature. Only dissimulated can (woman's) nature be loved. Like Zarathoustra, the somnambulist strives to reach the heights where he feels elevated high above profane nature and only then is free to pursue his lofty artistic contemplation. And like the Greeks, Nietzsche needs the Apollonian mask of the dream and the illusion in order for him to stomach Dionysus' horrific splendor.

The quintessential accomplishment for a woman is, for Nietzsche, to become a replica of the ideal male, who is heroic, lofty, sublime and royal.[78] In the play of perfect mimicry, woman may give voice to the sublime masculine soul, without difference. This could be achieved in the theatre where woman could give the impression of possessing such precious characteristics. However, it could only be achieved on one condition: that any trace of the maternal of the "housewifely" be completely erased. Thus, the aim is to create in woman an immaculate mimesis of the heroic male, devoid of any sexual difference.

Irigaray introduces the figure of Ariadne to illustrate this celebration of the perfected copy of the masculine. Like that of Athena, the myth of Ariadne speaks of the young maiden whose purpose it is to serve her father, Minos, and her man, Theseus. In the likeness of the spider, she incessantly spins the thread that Theseus uses to conquer the Minotaur by holding on to the thread and thus securing his safe return from the labyrinth. Nietzsche repeatedly celebrates the intelligence and inventiveness of Ariadne.[79] Yet nobody was capable of saving Ariadne from her destiny. After she had aided Theseus towards his glorious victory over the Minotaur, she was given to him by her father. But, alas, he left her alone on an island, and departed with her sister Phaedra as his new lover.

What is important for Irigaray about Nietzsche's hailing of Athena and Ariadne is that they are both young virgins whose greatness consists in the fact that they are replicas of the masculine. And, most importantly, they display no evidence of sexual difference. Their virtue lies in the fact that they can be viewed as doubles of the males. But in so doing, they separate from their own nature, which has to be cloaked in order for them to be objects of exchange between males. The hymen/marriage is always in play as the breaking-point between the one and the other, but always within the economy of the *same*:

> Since the current exchange rate is perhaps no more than a semblance on the inside of sameness, a passage from same to same. Which explains the need for disguises: cut between the male one and the other – the other of the same, that is – which would manage to establish relationships only by means of disguise. By an extra layer of dissimulation: that is loaded upon the woman. That the female is reduced to.[80]

Persephone, another young virgin, together with Athena and Ariadne, thus constitute the "hymen" between the two realms which man, in his alienation from himself, has created. As the intermediary between the two, the virgin is exchanged and is in that way dissimulated. The separation between the celestial and the terrestrial, the light and the dark, the truth and its reverse, reality and its shadow etc., finds the limit of demarcation in the figure of this intermediary young (wo)man. In this sense, Persephone is given by the god above, Zeus, to his brother, Hades, in an exchange that steals, veils, and violates her for the second time.

Her ignorance is the culprit. The daughter of Demeter, the goddess of the earth and the grain, Persephone has flourished as a young girl close to her mother's garden of fruits and flowers, and has been completely sheltered from death. With the arrival of Hades, this idyllic state is shattered, and she vanishes without a trace to the underworld. This abduction devastates Demeter, her mother, but she is unable to retrace her daughter behind the veil of death.

For Irigaray, the abduction signifies this forced separation, willed by the gods in the name of necessity, that steals the daughter away from the mother in order to impose death/phallus between the two, forcing the young girl to move from blissful ignorant virginity to the semblant and feigning world of femininity:

> Persephone – the voice snatched away to death, with no trace left of the kidnapping. From *Kore* to Persephone, the passage must be forgotten. From her to her(self) there must be no possible connection. Between the naturally virgin little girl and the robbed/raped woman – paralyzed in her becoming when she falls into an abyss alien to her: death for the men – the intervention of a pretense, of a semblance of femininity, would seem to prevent any turning back.[81]

Because she has traversed the line that demarcates the two realms, she has acquired a wisdom of the difference between the two. Thus, when she is reunited with her mother, she witnesses the flourishing of life of spring and summer that follows, but when she has to return to Hades, she experiences the death and barrenness of winter. This difference becomes for Irigaray one between proximity (to herself and to her mother) and propriety (her status as Hades' property) that exemplifies the difference between the will of the mother as opposed to the will of the father. In Irigaray's interpretation, the one means a life in abundance and growth whereas the other means a life of lack, of death and of deprivation of her freedom. Irigaray describes Persephone's life during the cold season as follows:

> Persephone becomes the ice being. Truth of any production that has been cut off from the natural world. Henceforward enslaved to a mirage technique that separates her from herself. Veiled without within, the *Kore* is arrested in her becoming. Immortally and never more a virgin.[82]

But this interpretation fails to take into account the tradition that exists of mythical and poetic figures who supposedly have made the same trip. Persephone is in privileged company as one of the few select who is admitted to traverse the limit. Only the poets, such as Homer, Ovid, Virgil, and Dante[83] have had the power to guide their heroes, Odysseus, Orpheus, Aeneas and Dante through the underworld. Persephone's virginal beauty is what gains her access to the forbidden realm for mortals, whereas Orpheus' music was what granted him access.

In each case, the characters, whether mythical or poetic, have gained access to the underworld and the unique insight that the journey provides because of their extra-ordinary qualities. A recurring theme that emerges in all of these stories, is the inevitability of death and the imposition of temporality on human life. Understood in this manner, Persephone's abduction to Hades seems to convey the impossibility of an idyllic temporal existence. The myth also seems to portray her life in the garden as a young girl as an existence that cannot last, but that she like every mortal has to enter into the world of temporality and by implication, of violence. Furthermore, Persephone's movement from one realm to another comes to mark the passing of time through the changing of the seasons, and therefore to be a part of nature, and not something that is hostile or foreign to it.

According to Irigaray, Persephone's insight might in fact give rise to a new plurality, outside the domain of the specular objective, and which circumvents the square as well as the circle. Persephone exceeds all horizons, but in her differentiated being she remains always familiar to the other, without appropriating it.

It is interesting to note Irigaray's attempt at undermining all of the constituents (world, the hermeneutic circle, horizon etc.) of the Heideggerian discourse on *Dasein*'s Being-in-the-world[84] in the following description of this new plurality that Persephone affirms:

> Thus is ceaselessly engendered the expression of her "world" that does not develop within any square or circle or... and remains without limit or boundary. Anything occurring in that world is wedded in movement, if it remains an other that self-embraces. Passive and active, feeling without feeling ressentiment. This rhythm, barely perceptible even to "small ears", subtends, nourishes, and accompanies others, like a background of air and light and warmth without appearing to do so. Tactile substrate destined to be forgotten, when the eye and the ear alone wish to marry/make merry.[85]

What Irigaray here affirms, is a rather far-reaching attack not only on Nietzsche's limited understanding of woman, but also an attack on all phenomenology of appearance, including Heidegger's. Her deconstruction of the multiple figurations of woman in Nietzsche show his complicity in the metaphysics of identity, presence and propriety, even when it finds expression in illusion, dream and art.

Furthermore, her reading of the privileged symbols of femininity such as the hysteric as well as the Greek goddesses Athena, Ariadne and Persephone reveal how woman has been enframed as that which she is not. Through a notion of femininity, woman's being ranged from connotations such as death, abyss, interval, intermediary, truth, untruth, lie, art, etc. However, what they all have failed to confront, is *le féminin* as the total potential of woman, which cannot be appropriated into any fixed form/idea. Nor can it be spoken in language.

While she has appropriated the Heideggerian path of inquiry in her attempt to deconstruct dominant modes of thinking about women, Irigaray eventually rejects what she considers to be his privileging of the *logos*, or as she formulates it, of language. In her view, Heidegger, like all of his predecessors, cannot confront woman's *mater-iality*, but insists on the transcendance of woman into some realm that deprives her of her fluidity and her multiplicity. The following quote from *L'oubli de l'air chez Martin Heidegger* seems to articulate Irigaray's quest for a sensitive immediacy that yet has to be explored and which still seems to incite fear in those who seek to unravel "the profound essence of the Dionysiac (*l'essence profonde du dionysiaque*)":

Does not being find its foundation in a sensible immediacy as yet unspoken? In a silence of that which secretly nourishes thought? The forbidden/unspoken and the undecidable in the relationship between man and nature which escapes his *logos*. Which gives itself (to be) in the unnamed site where the organs' contribution to all their meanings/senses gather. A given/gift which it projects in(to) a world and its objects. Thus recreating the whole, and making of everything the whole, and of the whole everyone, without the secret of this production ever being apparent to it.[86]

Marine Lover of Friedrich Nietzsche constitutes thus an attempt at invoking this dormant, silent, but still fecund resevoir of profound difference, namely the Dionysian woman, or, *le féminin*.

Conclusion

How, then, does Irigaray think sexual difference and the question of *le féminin* in the light of the nihilism problematic as it is thought by Nietzsche and Heidegger? Most (feminist) appropriations of Irigaray have been oblivious to this problematic as well as the broader philosophical implications of Irigaray's work. What seems to be the predominant preoccupation in most of the appropriations on which I focused in my first chapter, is the search for an effective methodology that can be applied in the quest for "woman".

In this respect, psychoanalysis has gained a privileged position, and most readings of Irigaray exclusively center on her psychoanalytic works and extract from them a critical methodology for reading other works. In my view, what is lost in this approach is any sensitivity to the philosophical inquiry in which Irigaray is engaged, that is, her interrogation of the philosophical tradition from Plato onwards in her pursuit of the question of sexual difference.

Furthermore, confusion reigns as to Irigaray's position vis-à-vis *mimesis* as it relates to the possibility of speaking the feminine (*parler femme*). Irigaray deconstructs the Platonic notion of *mimesis*, and even though she pursues a strategy of mimicking in her attempt to subvert what she considers to be the phal-logo-centric tradition, she never claims to have found a new language which mirrors *le féminin*. If this language exists at all, it is at best as a possibility that does not coincide with the logic of *mimesis* as it is thought by Plato onwards. Rather, *parler femme* cannot be contained within a specular logic, but exists as much in its absence as in its potential presence. Finally, what is completely silenced in these appropriations, is Irigaray's meditation on the Pre-Socratics and her attempt at retrieving the forgotten questions that these thinkers raised. In this context, she evokes the words *logos*, *aletheia* and *phusis* in her reading of what she calls "Nietzsche's oracular discourse".

Moreover, related to and in preparation for these appropriations, the question of appropriation *per se* was raised, which problematizes how anything "comes to be" in language and how it is subsequently present-ed to the inquiring subject for interpretation. Through Heidegger's notion of *Ereignis*, I opened up this grounding terrain to questioning. It revealed that "the event of appropriation" has remained unthought in all of these interpretations of Irigaray's work. By implication, the Being of the texts in question is never interrogated, but is instead taken for granted as something "ready-to-hand" that can be objectified and then scrutinized in terms of its ideological content, its "rhetoric" or its "value" as a "different" discourse within the institutional technology of academia.

Due to a consistent skirting of the ontological questions that ground any interpretative endeavor, I felt the need, in my second chapter, to address in greater detail the theoretical preliminaries connected to these problems. Therefore, by approaching the question of "woman" in terms of the inextricable link between "woman" and the postmodern notion of *écriture* as posited by Jacques Derrida, I discussed the ensuing implications for the question of sexual difference when confronted with this new philosophical terrain.

The problem of interpretation was furthermore outlined by showing how it is predicated upon an ontological *pre-understanding* that circumspectively understands in a fore-having, prior to any interpretative exposition. Finally, in an in-depth study of the nihilism problematic, I addressed the major rubrics of Nietzsche's thinking on nihilism as well as Heidegger's meditation on Nietzsche as exemplified in his "mighty tome", *Nietzsche*.

When Nietzsche thinks nihilism at the end of the 19th century, he predicts the epistemological crisis that is about to happen and through his astute analysis, he foresees the *malaise* of modernity that follows. For Nietzsche, however, nihilism means "the devaluation of all values", which in its destructive stance obliterates the certitude that allowed the philosopher of the past to make universal claims. The remedy to this impotence is the Nietzschean overman who affirms a *new* position, based on his own perspectival subjectivity which artistically appropriates the world in "a grand style".

In his *Nihilism* volume on Nietzsche, Heidegger demonstrates, however, that Nietzsche's attempt at overcoming metaphysics through his *transvaluative* stance still confines him within the metaphysics that he attempts to overcome. By positing a Cartesian subjectivity that *wills through valuation*, Nietzsche initiates a new metaphysics, which Heidegger calls a metaphysics of valuation. In my treatment of Nietzsche, I align myself with Heidegger's assessment of the problem, and in so doing, I delineate the Heideggerian meditation on the essential connectedness between Nietzsche and Descartes, despite Nietzsche's own refutation of Descartes' philosophy.

It is within the problematic of nihilism that I approach, in my third chapter, Irigaray's reading of Nietzsche's *Thus Spoke Zarathoustra* in her work *Marine Lover of Friedrich Nietzsche*. Irigaray initiates "a lover's discourse" with Nietzsche, in which she attempts to listen in on his most muted language in *Zarathoustra*. She thereby tries to decipher that which has been silenced in his writings, namely the foundational ground on which he erects his philosophy of will to power. What is at stake is not so much what "stands there" in terms of textual evidence; rather Irigaray seeks to find that within Nietzsche which he himself could not decipher, namely the "immemorial waters" from which everything emerges.

This absence is thought by Irigaray in terms of a symbolic murder of the (M)Other, the matrix, or, the elemental (amniotic) waters from whence all living beings originate. Furthermore, Irigaray shows that, in his frantic endeavor to repress and deny his primordial connectedness to this *locus*, the philosopher has erected a philosophic language that alienates him from this matrix while positing his own self-engendering within a transcendental realm.

Even though Nietzsche criticizes the metaphysical tradition which claims to have separated the man of reason from his elemen-

tal and material being, his own transvaluation of "woman's materiality" as the untruth of truth, still remains fixed within the Platonic paradigm which he ventures to undo. According to Irigaray,
by projecting the concentric circle of the subject that wills power,
Nietzsche's overman attempts to appropriate every being within his
own perspectival subjectivity, and in so doing, he simultaneously
expels the (M)Other.

Moreover, in his pursuit of the "higher man", Nietzsche projects an elevated and lofty world in which Zarathoustra reigns.[1] In
his flight to the mountains and in his quest for the eternal return of
the same, Irigaray sees Nietzsche as being a complice in the denial
of, and the escape from, the elemental (mother) earth that made his
birth possible. Zarathoustra declares his love to eternity, as the
only "woman" that he could love. In so doing, Irigaray interprets
Nietzsche as shunning that which woman is in her natural element.[2] Instead, he is completely enamored by his own narcissistic
projections. Consequently, he is deaf to Echo's declaration of love
for him. Perhaps like Echo's tragic love for Narcissus, Irigaray's
"lover's discourse" to Nietzsche falls on deaf ears?

But in Irigaray's insertion of the forgotten ground in Nietzsche's
thinking by calling on the profound *logos* of the absent nocturnal
immemorial waters which she posits as the (M)Other matrix, I read
an attempt at raising an ontological question. In so doing, she
equates the withdrawal of the (M)Other with Heideggers's notion
of the withdrawal of Being while evoking the Pre-Socratic notion
phusis, which was the word through which the Pre-Socratics
thought all emergent beings. However, due to the Roman appropriation of *phusis* in the first century A.D., which translated this
word as *natura*, part of the Pre-Socratic meditation is lost. Consequently, Irigaray comes to understand the (M)Other as this lost
ontological ground as "that which gives birth" in the Roman sense
of *natura*. What she inadvertently does in the process, is to name
that which cannot be named, namely Being. As a result, the
(M)Other as a potential ontological ground becomes metaphysical
through and through.

As such, the (M)Other represents a transvaluated value that has
been *willfully* silenced and suppressed by a sworn conspiracy
among the long line of philosophers that predate Irigaray, includ-

ing Nietzsche. Irigaray diagnoses the cause of this deficiency to be in a *subjective error*. This is where Irigaray's meditation on the ontological ground of Nietzsche's thinking departs most radically from that of Heidegger. In Heidegger's view, the withdrawal of Being as the ground for all emergents, is not effected by the subject, but is rather a default of Being itself. That is, Being is *as* beings precisely in the withdrawal of Being itself. And, most importantly, this state of affairs cannot be caused nor remedied by the human subject, since Being is what gives this subject a being through this default.

In my fourth Chapter, I perform an in-depth interrogation of Irigaray's reading of Nietzsche's positing of "woman" as "the untruth of truth". She radically differs from Nietzsche's basic presupposition that "nothing is more foreign to woman than truth" by claiming that "untruth" is never foreign to truth, but rather *proper to it* as an extension of the logic of the *same*.

In her chapter called *"Lèvres violées"*, Irigaray carefully examines selected aphorisms from *Beyond Good and Evil*, *The Gay Science*, *Twilight of the Idols* and *The Birth of Tragedy* which speak to the question of "woman" and "truth". Nietzsche's argument rests predominantly on the above assertion in which woman comes to represent the simulacrum, beauty or illusion that is truth's "other". Irigaray convincingly uncovers how this duplicates, even when it reverses, the Platonic division between "truth" and "illusion", a schema which has objectified "woman" within a binary opposition of difference that has *nothing* to say about how woman might differ *in herself*.

By being relegated to a host of signifiers, "woman" has come to signify all that which she is not, and which he has attempted to expel from his own being. Consequently, "woman" has been represented *as that which she is not*, namely "femininity". Thought within the Nietzschean duality of the Apollonian and the Dionysian, "woman" represents for Nietzsche the incarnation of the magic of the Apollonian mask of illusion. By viewing "femininity" as the (un)truth of "woman", Nietzsche is horrified when he fathoms what her *nature* might be. Therefore, he prefers to contemplate her in her (projected) beauty, but *at a distance*. For Irigaray, "woman" thus defined only becomes yet another signifier that has been attributed to "woman" in the history of Western metaphysics. As such, it is not much different from those signifiers that she has been given prior to Nietzsche.

In my assessment of Irigaray's argument, I evoke the Heideggerian intertext of the "*as*-structure", which I believe enters into Irigaray's thinking on the figuration of "woman" *as* that which she is not. According to Irigaray, because all of Western metaphysics has always already been appropriated by the masculine, "woman" can only speak in the absences and blind spots[3] that evoke the traces of an "elsewhere" in that language. As that which is totally foreign to the economy of truth, unity and mastery, Irigaray projects this "elsewhere" in *le féminin*.

Given the oculocentrism of our philosophical tradition in general and of phenomenology in particular, Irigaray envisages *le féminin* to reside outside this privileging of the "visible". In this sense, she deliberately attempts to circumvent phenomenology, including that of Heidegger. However, in her attempt at thinking that which does not appear, but which withdraws in its own coming to be, Heidegger's meditation on the "*as*-structure" seems to have become a different avenue that opens up the possibility of thinking *le féminin*.

Le féminin thus becomes the *undecidable* which defies (self-)identity, and which thus challenges the entire foundation for our metaphysical language. Bereft of subjective identity, representational language cannot deliver its object of mastery. Therefore, in its subversive (non)being, *le féminin* signifies the death of the subject. However, according to Irigaray, that does not exhaust its (non)being. Rather, *le féminin* subsists underlying all discursivity as "*matière première*".

It is in this sense that Irigaray's thinking resides in the proximity of that of Heidegger. Like *le féminin*, Being can never assume any identity, but in its unfolding in the clearing of history, it will always be appropriated by tradition and thereby always appear *as* beings in its ontological *difference* from Being. Furthermore, both Heidegger and Irigaray emphasize this ontological difference, which in Irigaray's terminology is expressed in the difference between "*matière première*" and (visible) "*formes*". But whereas Irigaray's discourse pays heed to the figure of the (M)Other as the form-engendering force, Heidegger instead emphasizes the "gift" given by Being in presenting whatever appears in *language*.

When it comes to woman's nature, all has yet to be discovered, claims Irigaray. In her reading of Nietzsche's *The Birth of Tragedy*, she resurrects the Nietzschean notion of the Dionysian, but by divorcing it from its dependency on the Apollonian. In so doing, she projects the horrific and destructive aspect of *le féminin* through a revised notion of Dionysus. By returning to the Greek tragedies, and in particular to Aeschylus' *Oresteia*, Irigaray attempts to retrieve the hidden vestige of *le féminin* through the figure of Dionysus.

In Irigaray's re-reading, the mythic and tragic figures from this remote past remind us of the primordial *strife* that took place among the Greeks in terms of the question of sexual difference. By carefully scrutinizing the Olympian gods[4] and the function within this mythology of the younger gods, Athena and Apollo, Irigaray shows how sexual difference is eradicated in these figures, how they both speak and represent the *law of the father*, Zeus. As a copy of the masculine, Athena (and for that matter Ariadne) embodies the patriarchal order in its denial and murder of the (M)Other.

Only in the young virgin goddess Persephone does Irigaray identify a resonance of the primordial goddess Gaia and her chthonic allies, the Furies. Not only does the destiny of the young abducted Persephone exemplify the destiny of "woman" in the West and her "*lèvres violées*", but her figure also embodies what might be nominated Irigaray's ideal: a *difference within*. Persephone knows the realm of death and its ruler, Hades, but at the same time, she knows and acknowledges her love for and her loyalty to the world of appearances and her mother, Demeter. In her superior knowledge, she traverses *both* realms, and in her movement, temporality unfolds.

It is my contention that the Heideggerian meditation on the Pre-Socratic words *logos*, *aletheia* and *phusis* in addition to his thinking on the question of the ontological difference form some of the most important inter-texts in Irigaray's writing on sexual difference. I have attempted to uncover the basic constituents of her reading of Nietzsche (and Heidegger) and thereby to point to the way in which the Heideggerian inquiry has provided an avenue to think the question of sexual difference differently.

In Irigaray's reading of Nietzsche, she follows in his path when it comes to his appropriation of Plato. As I have previously noted in a footnote in Chapter IV,[5] most of Nietzsche's philosophy rests on this basic assumption that there exists in Plato a "raging discord" between "art" and "truth". However, as Heidegger shows in this quote, Plato's word *eidos* has not been thoroughly exhausted in terms of its potential meanings. Traditionally, in metaphysical language it has come to represent "the idea(l)" in its (non)-visible form. What Heidegger suggests, however, is that Plato also names in the word *eidos* "that which constitutes the essence in the audible, the tasteable, the tactile, in anything that is in any way accessible".[6]

What this quote implies for my project, is the possibility it opens up for a new reading of Plato in the sense that it undermines the traditional opposition that has been erected between the sensuous and the supra-sensuous, between the visible and the non-visible. This reading would in turn seriously compromise Irigaray's reading of Nietzsche, which rests within the same appropriation of Plato.

If we were to pursue the implications of this startling reading of Plato, what would happen to the question of sexual difference such as it has been posited by Irigaray? Would her whole premise crumble, that is, that in Western metaphysics there has been a denial and a repression of the (M)Other thought as the material matrix that allows everything to be? Could it be that language has already appropriated her thinking into a path out of which she cannot will herself and which it might take centuries to undo? Or, could it be that nihilism, as the "history of Being" has finally caught up with her project and thus plunged *le féminin* into the abysmal nothing to which all beings are eventually destined?

Notes

Introduction

1. Luce Irigaray, "Sexual Difference", trans. Seán Hand, in Margaret Whitford, ed. *The Irigaray Reader* (Oxford: Basil Blackwell, 1991), p. 165.
2. Martin Heidegger, *Being and Time*, trans. John Macquarrie & Edward Robinson (New York: Harper & Row, 1962), pp. 24–25. All subsequent references to Heidegger will be made to available English translations of his work.
3. "Sexual Difference", p. 165.
4. Ibid., p. 166.
5. Luce Irigaray, *Speculum de l'autre femme* (Paris: Les Éditions de Minuit, 1974). All references will be made to the English translation, *Speculum of the Other Woman*, trans. Gillian C. Gill (Ithaca: Cornell University Press, 1985). This quote is taken from the opening of the section entitled "Speculum", p. 133.
6. See "Le genre féminin" in *Sexes et parentés* (Paris: Les Éditions de Minuit, 1987), pp. 119–138.
7. Most academic disciplines are still governed by instrumental thinking based on assertive and deductive logic, and the dominant mode of this book will inevitably be both descriptive and representational. Within this frame of thought, the comfortable categories such as author, text, consciousness etc., are taken for granted, and become the secure references upon which a "sound" argumentation rests. Even though attempts will be made to work against the grain of this prescribed logic, I will likewise be forced to operate within this imaginary field of delimitation.
8. Luce Irigaray, *Ce sexe qui n'en est pas un* (Paris: Les Éditions de Minuit, 1977). All references will be made to the English translation of this work by Catherine Porter and Carolyn Burke, *This Sex Which Is Not One* (Ithaca: Cornell University Press, 1985).
9. Jacques Lacan, "The mirror stage as formative of the function of the I as revealed in psychoanalytic experience", trans. Alan Sheridan (New York: Norton, 1977), pp. 1–7.
10. *Speculum*, p. 142.
11. "Sexual Difference", *The Irigaray Reader*, pp. 165–166.
12. Luce Irigaray, *Amante marine de Friedrich Nietzsche* (Paris: Les Éditions de Minuit, 1980). All subsequent references will be made to the Gillian C.

Gill's English translation of the book, *Marine Lover of Friedrich Nietzsche* (New York: Columbia University Press, 1991).

13. My reading will be based on the concept of *intertextuality* as it is introduced by Julia Kristeva in "Revolution in Poetic Language" in *The Kristeva Reader*, ed. Toril Moi (Oxford: Basil Blackwell, 1986), p. 111:

   The term *intertextuality* denotes this transposition of one (or several) sign-system(s) into another; but since this term has often been understood in the banal sense of "study of sources", we prefer the term *transposition* because it specifies that the passage from one signifying system to another demands a new articulation of the thetic – of enunciative and denotative positionality.

14. In *Le corps-à-corps avec la mère* (Montréal: Les Éditions de la pleine lune, 1981) Irigaray hints at what this path might be when she makes the following statement (pp. 45–46):

   Je dirais que dans la parole de *Zarathoustra*, la parole est beaucoup plus oraculaire [que celui de Platon], qu'elle se rapproche de certaines paroles présocratiques, que de ce qui est entendu aujourd'hui comme fiction.

   My translation:

   I would say that in Zarathoustra's speech, language is much more oracular [than that of Plato], that it comes close to certain Pre-Socratic words, that which today is understood as fiction.

15. See Friedrich Nietzsche, *The Will to Power*, trans. Walter Kaufmann (New York: Vintage Books, 1967), p. 9. All subsequent references will be made to Kaufmann's English translations of Nietzsche's works.

16. The concept of transvaluation in Nietzsche is perhaps best illuminated in *Thus Spoke Zarathoustra*, trans. Walter Kaufmann in *The Portable Nietzsche* (New York: The Viking Press, 1968), pp. 103–442.

17. Martin Heidegger, "Letter on Humanism", in *Martin Heidegger: Basic Writings*, trans. Frank A. Capuzzi, ed. Davis Farrell Krell (New York: Harper & Row, 1977), p. 213.

18. Luce Irigaray, *Sexes et parentés* (Paris: Les Éditions de Minuit, 1987), p. 107:

   C'est probablement à cette conception du lien entre le sujet et le langage que Jacques Lacan a pris sa définition de l'inconscient. L'expression "L'inconscient est structuré comme un langage" est bien proche de celle de Martin Heidegger: "L'homme se comporte comme s'il était le créateur et le maître du langage, alors que c'est celui-ci au contraire qui est et demeure son souverain." (cf. "L'Homme habite en poète", dans *Chemins*, Gallimard, 1962).

   The translation is my own (except the reference to Heidegger from *Poetry, Language, Thought*). In cases where there are no translations available in English, I refer to the French texts. If I provide my own translation, I also include the quote in the original.

19. Luce Irigaray, *Éthique de la différence sexuelle* (Paris: Les Éditions de Minuit, 1984), p. 122:

   Le langage, pour formel qu'il soit, s'est nourri de sang, de chair, d'éléments matériels. Qui et quoi l'a nourri? Comment payer cette dette?

Devons-nous produire des mécanismes de plus en plus formels, tech-
niques, qui se retournent contre l'homme, tel l'aboutissement inversé de
cette mère qui lui a donné un corps vivant? Et qu'il craint à la mesure de
l'impayé entre elle et lui.
20. See Martin Heidegger and Eugene Fink, *Heraclitus Seminar: 1966/67*,
    trans. Charles H. Seibert (Alabama: University of Alabama Press, 1982).
21. *Being and Time*, pp. 149–168.
22. Jacques Lacan, "Traduction de 'Logos' de Heidegger", *La Psychanalyse*, 1
    (1956), pp. 59–79.
23. See Luce Irigaray, *Le langage des déments* (Paris: Éditions Mouton,
    1973); *Parler n'est jamais neutre* (Paris: Les Éditions de Minuit, 1985);
    and ed. Luce Irigaray, *Sexes et genres à travers les langues: éléments de
    communication sexuée* (Paris: Grasset, 1991).

Chapter 1

1. In the wake of Post-structuralism and its critique of "identity", feminists
   have become increasingly reluctant to embrace this category in fear of
   becoming easy targets for attacks which would label them as
   "metaphysicians of presence". Traditional denominations such as
   "feminist", which were based on the integrity and solidity of the thinking
   (political) subject, does not take into account any excess and difference
   that might exceed the boundaries of such an identity.
2. Jane Gallop, *The Daughter's Seduction: Feminism and Psychoanalysis*
   (Ithaca: Cornell University Press, 1982).
3. See Elizabeth L. Berg, "The Third Woman", *Diacritics* (Summer 1982),
   12, p. 16.
4. Toril Moi, *Sexual/Textual Politics* (New York: Methuen, 1985), pp.
   127–149.
5. See Margaret Whitford, *Luce Irigaray: Philosophy in the Feminine*
   (London: Routledge, 1991); ed. Margaret Whitford, *The Irigaray Reader*
   (Oxford: Basil Blackwell, 1991) and Margaret Whitford, "Speaking as a
   woman: Luce Irigaray and the female imaginary." *Radical Philosophy* 21:
   18–28.
6. See Elizabeth Gross, "Philosophy, subjectivity and the body: Kristeva and
   Irigaray" in E. Grosz and Pateman, eds, *Feminist Challenges: Social and
   Political Theory* (Sydney: Allen & Unwin, 1986) pp. 125–43; Elizabeth
   Gross, "Irigaray and sexual difference" *Australian Feminist Studies* 2
   (Autumn 1986) 63–77; Elizabeth Gross, "Irigaray and the divine" *Local
   Consumption Papers*, no. 9; Elizabeth Gross, "Derrida, Irigaray and
   deconstruction", in "Leftwright", *Intervention* 20 (1986) 70–81; Elizabeth
   Grosz, "Notes towards a corporal feminism", *Australian Feminist Studies*
   5 (Summer 1987) 1–16; Elizabeth Grosz, "Desire, the body and recent
   French feminisms, *Intervention* 21–22 (1988) 28–33; Elizabeth Grosz,

Sexual Subversions: Three French Feminists (Sydney: Allen & Unwin, 1989).

7. Naomi Schor, "This Essentialism Which Is Not One", *differences* 1 (2); 33–58.

8. See Margaret Whitford, "Luce Irigaray and the Female Imaginary: Speaking as a Woman", *Radical Philosophy* (Summer 1986), 43, p. 3.

9. See Sherry Turkle for an in depth account of the polemics between Irigaray and Lacan in *Psychoanalytic Politics: Freud's French Revolution* (Cambridge, Massachusetts: The MIT Press, 1978).

10. See Heidegger's essay "The End of Metaphysics and the Task of Thinking" in *On Time and Being*, trans. Joan Staumbach (New York: Harper & Row, 1969), pp. 55–73.

11. See for example Denise Riley, "Does Sex Have a History" *New Formations* (Spring 1987); Stanton, Domna C., "Difference on Trial: A Critique of the Maternal Metaphor in Cixous, Irigaray, and Kristeva", in *The Poetics of Gender*, ed. Nancy K. Miller (New York: Columbia University Press, 1986).

12. This is particularly true within the more politically oriented faction of the feminist movement. In this context, names like Monique Wittig, Monique Plaza and other contributors to the journal *Feminist Issues* have taken the lead in warning against what they perceive to be Irigaray's excessive intellectualization of the problem and her so-called a-historical approach.

13. See "This Essentialism Which Is Not One", where she elaborates on these different forms of essentialism, which she nominates the "Liberationist Critique", the "Linguistic Critique", the "Metaphysical Critique" and the "Feminist Critique" respectively.

14. See Toril Moi in *Sexual/Textual Politics*, p. 139:

    Deconstruction is in other words self-confessedly parasitic upon the metaphysical discourses it is out to subvert. It follows that any attempt to formulate a general theory of femininity will be metaphysical. This is precisely Irigaray's dilemma: having shown that so far femininity has been produced exclusively in relation to the logic of the Same, she falls for the temptation to produce her own positive theory of femininity. But, as we have seen, to define "woman" is necessarily to essentialize her.

15. See Heidegger's meditation on the question of history and its primordial connectedness to temporality in *Being and Time*, pp. 427–428:

    If the question of historicality leads us back to these "sources", then the *locus* of the problem of history has already been decided. This *locus* is not to be sought in historiology as the science of history. Even if the problem of "history" is treated in accordance with a theory of science, not only aiming at the "epistemological" clarification of the historiological way of grasping things (Simmel) or at the logic with which the concepts of historiological presentation are formed (Rickert), but doing so with an orientation towards "the side of the object", then as long as the question is formulated this way, history becomes in principle accessible only as the *Object* of science. Thus the basic phenomenon of history, which is prior to any thematizing by historiology and underlies it, has been irretrievably put aside. How history can become a possible *object* for historiology is something that may be gathered only from the kind of Being which belongs to the historical – from historicality, and from the way it is rooted in temporality.

16. Most "political" discourses, and particularly Marxist discourse, posit ideology as the ground for **all** discursive practices. In this respect, there is a projection of a "contextual base", usually expressed in the triad, the "historical", the "economic" and the "political". What remains unthought in this interpretation, is the ontological understanding on which this triad rests. Irigaray's contribution might in part be attributed to the fact that she calls for a return to the ontological problematic, which reveals how "Marxism", "Feminism" or any other -ism has always already been pre-written in the philosophical language and its major philosophemes. Therefore, if change is to occur, there has to be enacted an intervention in relation to this ontological ground. Whether this is possible or how it will be done, are questions which she diligently pursues.

17. "This Essentialism", p. 19.

18. *This Sex*, p. 76.

19. It is interesting to note that Irigaray has become the privileged figure within this new proliferation of readings that appropriate her writings as a *method* to read everything from Plato, the Medieval Mystics, Shakespeare to H.D. The following list provides references to a selection of articles which all *use* Irigaray in terms of a new reading strategy that claims to have discovered "difference:":

Barbara Freeman, "Irigaray at *The Symposium*: Speaking Otherwise", *Oxford Literary Review* 8, (1986), Nos. 1–2: *Sexual Difference*;

Shirley Neuman, "Importing Difference" in *Amazing Space: Canadian Women Writing*, eds. Shirley Neuman and Smaro Kamboureli (Edmonton: Longspoon Press, 1986);

Eve Kosofsky Sedgewick, *Between Men: English Literature and Male Homosexual Desire* (New York: Columbia University Press, 1985);

Patricia Parker, *Literary Fat Ladies: Rhetoric, Gender, Property* (London: Methuen, 1987);

Sara Beckwith, "A Very Material Mysticism: the Medieval Mysticism of Margery Kempe" in *Medieval Literature: Criticism, Ideology, and History* (New York: St. Martin Press, 1986);

Elizabeth A. Hirsh, "H.D., Modernism, and the Psychoanalysis of Seeing", *Literature and Psychology*, 32, 3 (1986), pp. 1–10.

20. *Ereignis* is usually translated as "the event of appropriation", and as such it has been the target of much debate. This translation might in fact be somewhat misleading. In *On Time and Being*, Heidegger warns against how *Ereignis* must **not** be thought (p. 20):

What the name "event of Appropriation" names can no longer be represented by means of the current meaning of the word; for in that meaning "event of Appropriation" is understood in the sense of occurrence and happening – not in terms of Appropriating as the extending and sending which opens and preserves.

21. *On Time and Being*, pp. 12–13.
22. In Lacanian psychoanalysis, for example, the Other or the unconscious is thought in terms of the privative, as that which does not appear, but which nevertheless enters into the unfolding of the "now". In this sense, Lacan is interested in considering the unconscious, not as an entity, but as a process of disclosure. The Being of the unconscious thus comes to signify the disclosure of Dasein conceived as a presence made up of absence. This interpretation of Lacan's "Dasein psychoanalysis" has sometimes been attributed to his early work, especially in connection to his work *The Language of the Self: The Function of Language in Psychoanalysis*, trans. Anthony Wilden (New York: Delta Books, 1968).
23. *On Time and Being*, p. 14.
24. Ibid., p. 14.
25. Ibid., pp. 15–16.
26. Ibid., pp. 21–22.
27. Heidegger here develops Immanuel Kant's understanding of *a priori*, which he defines in his *Critique of Pure Reason*, trans. Norman Kemp Smith (New York: St. Martin Press, 1929). In the following, Kant emphasizes the *a priori* as the inner necessity, a sensible intuition of space and time (p. 67):

In the course of this investigation it will be found there are two pure forms of sensible intuition, serving as principles of *a priori* knowledge, namely space and time.

28. Ibid., pp. 22–23.
29. *Being and Time*, pp. 279–311.
30. In *The Question Concerning Technology*, trans. William Lowitt. (New York: Harper & Row, 1977), Heidegger defines the word *Gestell* (p. 20):

According to ordinary usage, the word *Gestell* [frame] means some kind of apparatus, e.g. a bookrack. *Gestell* is also the name for a skeleton. And the employment of the word *Ge-stell* [Enframing] that is now required of us seems equally eerie, not to speak of the arbitrariness with which words of a mature language.

Heidegger furthermore elaborates on his selection of this word in the following (p.21):

The word *stellen* [to set upon] in the name *Ge-stell* [Enframing] not only means challenging. At the same time it should preserve the suggestion of another *Stellen* from which it stems, namely, that producing and presenting [*Her- und Dar-stellen*] which, in the sense of *poiesis*, lets what presences come forth – e.g., the erecting of a statue in the temple precinct – and the challenging ordering now under consideration are indeed fundamentally different, and yet they remain related in their essence. Both are ways of revealing, of *aletheia*. In Enframing, that unconcealment comes to pass in conformity with which the work of modern technology reveals the real as standing-reserve. This work is therefore neither only a human activity nor a mere means within this activity. The merely instrumental, merely anthropological definition of technology is therefore in principle untenable. And it cannot be rounded out by being referred back to some metaphysical or religious explanation that undergrids it.

31. Martin Heidegger, *On the Way To Language*, trans. Peter D. Hertz (New York: Harper & Row, 1971), p. 35.

32. See Jean Baudrillard for an excellent analysis of the workings of modern cybernetics and its relationship to homogenized information through the development of a mass culture of mass-produced "knowledge" in *Simulations*, trans. Paul Foss et al. (New York: Semiotext(e) Inc., 1983).

33. In regard to the field of literary criticism, it is possible to subsume the Russian Formalists, the Prague School, Julia Kristeva, the Tel Quelians as well as Todorov into this group of theorists who sought to formalize language and to make it an object of study.

34. See *On the Way To Language*, p. 134.

35. Ibid., p. 135.

36. See Lacan's understanding of the subject's entrance into the symbolic order as an order that always pre-exists us and into which we are necessarily *subjected* in order to be in language.

Chapter II

1. Jacques Derrida, *Spurs: Nietzsche's Styles/Éperons: Les Styles de Nietzsche* (Chicago: The University of Chicago Press, 1978).

2. Ibid., p. 71.

3. Ibid., p. 57.

4. See Alice A. Jardine, *Gynesis: Configurations of Woman and Modernity* (Ithaca: Cornell University Press, 1985). In her chapter called "The Woman-in-effect", Jardine explores the new configurations of woman and modernity. I quote:

   Woman, as a new rhetorical space, is inseparable from the most radical moments of most contemporary disciplines. To limit ourselves to the general set of writers in focus here, "she" may be found in Lacan's pronouncements of desire; Derrida's internal explorations of writing; Deleuze's work on becoming woman; Jean-François Lyotard calls for a feminine analytic relation; Jean Baudrillard's work on seduction; Foucault's on madness; Goux's on the new femininity; Barthes's in general; Michel Serres's desire to become Penelope or Ariadne [...] "She" is created from the close explorations of semantic chains whose elements have changed textual as well as conceptual positions, at least in terms of a valorization: from time to space, the same to other, paranoia to hysteria, city to labyrinth, mastery to nonmastery, truth to fiction. (p. 38)

5. Jacques Derrida, *Positions*, trans. Alan Bass (Chicago: The University of Chicago Press, 1981), p. 26.

6. Derrida's thinking on the "always-already-structure" is somewhat analogous to Heidegger's notion of a "fore-having", and will be dealt with in greater detail later in the chapter under the question of pre-understanding. The major difference between the two, however, seems to lie in the fact

that Derrida operates within a psychoanalytic framework as a foundational discourse, and the "always-already" seems to, in some way, structurally be related to Freud's notion of the unconscious. This is perhaps best illustrated in his work on Freud's magic writing-pad in "Freud and the Scene of Writing" in *Writing and Difference*, trans. Alan Bass (Chicago: The University of Chicago Press, 1978), pp. 196–231.

7. See Jacques Derrida, "Freud and the Scene of Writing" in *Writing and Difference*, trans. Alan Bass (Chicago: University of Chicago Press, 1978), pp. 196–231.
8. *Spurs*, p. 73.
9. Ibid., p. 73.
10. Martin Heidegger, *Being and Time* (New York: Harper & Row, 1962), p. 191.
11. Ibid., p. 192.
12. Ibid., p. 189.
13. Ibid., p. 194.
14. Ibid., p. 195.
15. Ibid., p. 199.
16. Ibid., p. 200.
17. Ibid., p. 201.
18. See Martin Heidegger's *Early Greek Thinking*, trans. David Farrell Krell and Frank A. Capuzzi (New York: Harper & Row, 1975).
19. Ibid., p. 202.
20. Friedrich Nietzsche, *The Will to Power* ed. and trans. Walter Kaufmann (New York: Vintage Books, 1967).
21. Ibid., p. 9.
22. Friedrich Nietzsche, *Thus Spoke Zarathoustra*, in *The Portable Nietzsche*, trans. and ed. Walter Kaufmann (New York: The Viking Press, 1968), pp. 103–439.
23. *The Will to Power*, p. 7.
24. Ibid., p. 7.
25. Martin Heidegger, *Nietzsche*. Volume IV: *Nihilism*, trans. David Farrell Krell (New York: Harper & Row, 1982).
26. Ibid., p. 4.
27. Ibid., p. 200.
28. Ibid., p. 200.
29. *The Will to Power*, p. 13.
30. Ibid., p. 17.
31. Ibid., p. 407.
32. Ibid., p. 14.
33. *Zarathoustra*, p. 96.
34. The Will to Power, p. 289.
35. Ibid., pp. 35–36.
36. *Zarathoustra*, p. 125.
37. Ibid., pp. 126–127.
38. *Nihilism*, p. 6.
39. Ibid., p. 9.

40. Ibid., p. 10.
41. In fact, Heidegger claims that this was the phrase that sparkled his interest in Nietzsche's thought and which initiated what was to become a decade of meditation on Nietzsche.
42. Ibid., p. 53.
43. Ibid., p. 83.
44. Ibid., p. 86.
45. Ibid., p. 100.
46. Ibid., pp. 104–105.
47. Ibid., p. 107.
48. Ibid., p. 108.
49. Ibid., p. 121.
50. Ibid., p. 134.
51. Ibid., p. 219.
52. Ibid., p. 221.
53. Ibid., p. 225.

Chapter III

1. See also Luce Irigaray, *Passions élémentaires* (Paris: Les Éditions de Minuit, 1982). In this work, Irigaray poetically explores the passions in their elemental nature as an expression of the cosmic connection between the body and the four elements: air, fire, water and earth.
2. These same figures likewise take center stage in *Speculum of the Other Woman*.
3. *Marine lover*, p. 3.
4. Ovid, *Metamorphoses*, trans. Rolfe Humphries (Bloomington: Indiana University Press, 1955), p. 68.
5. Ibid., p. 69.
6. *Speculum*, p. 264.
7. Irigaray develops this thought of the invisible air in *L'oubli de l'air chez Martin Heidegger*. She argues that Heidegger has forgotten the elemental air as that which nourishes all emergent, including language.
8. *Marine Lover*, p. 4.
9. Ibid., p. 4.
10. Ibid., p. 4.
11. Ibid., p. 5.
12. Ibid., p. 5.
13. Ibid., p. 5.
14. See also Hélène Cixous, "The Laugh of the Medusa", trans. Keith and Paula Cohen in *New French Feminisms*, eds. I. de Courtivron & E. Marks (New York, Shocken Books, 1981), pp. 245–265.
15. *Zarathoustra*, p. 122.
16. *Marine Lover*, p. 6.
17. Ibid., p. 6.

18. Ibid., p. 7.
19. Jacques Derrida, *Dissemination*, trans. Barbara Johnson (Chicago: University of Chicago Press, 1981), pp. 212–213.
20. *Marine Lover*, p. 7.
21. Irigaray plays on the homonym between the "entre" (between) end the "antre" (cave/womb) in "Plato's *Hystera*" in *Speculum*.
22. See *Spurs*, p. 71.
23. *Nihilism*, p. 210.
24. *Nihilism*, p. 192.
25. Ibid., p. 193.
26. *Marine Lover*, pp. 7–8.
27. Ibid., p. 9.
28. *Zárathoustra*, p. 340.
29. *Marine Lover*, p. 23.
30. Ibid., p. 10.
31. Ibid., p. 9.
32. Ibid., p. 9.
33. Ibid., p. 11.
34. Ibid., p. 11.
35. Freud, who experimented with the model which preceded that of Nietzsche, namely the mathematical-logical model initiated by the Greeks, ended up with the third model, the thermo-dynamic model. He borrowed his concept of a "complex" from this scientific field. The energy theory on which thermodynamics is based can be outlined in the following shorthand: first, the conservation of energy; second, a tendency towards death. In his work *Beyond the Pleasure Principle*, trans. James Strachey (New York: Norton, 1959) Freud speaks of this tendency in the following statement (p. 32):
    If we are to take it as a truth that knows no exception that everything living dies for *internal* reasons – becomes inorganic once again – then we shall be compelled to say that *the aim of all life is death* and, looking backwards, that *inanimate things existed before living ones.*
36. *The Ethics of Sexual Difference*, trans. Carolyn Burke. Ithaca: Cornell University Press. (Forthcoming)
37. *Éthique*, p. 120:
    La *science psychoanalytique* s'appuie sur les deux premiers principes de la thermodynamique, qui sous-tendent le modèle de la libido selon Freud. Or ces deux principes apparaissent plus isomorphes à la sexualité masculine que féminine. Celle-ci étant moins soumise aux alternances de tension-décharge, à la conservation de l'énergie requise, au maintien d'états d'equilibre, au fonctionnement en circuit clos et rouvert par saturation, à la réversibilité du temps, etc.
38. Irigaray refers to the Belgian Nobel laureate in Chemistry, Ilya Prigogine (1917–), who has developed a critique of the second law of thermodynamics. Prigogine's reinterpretation proposes that "in conditions that are sufficiently far from equilibrium, fluctuations of order in random system could suddenly stabilize. The resulting 'dissipative structures' – the most

dramatic of which is life itself – would last indefinitely, taking energy out
of the environments and 'dissipating' entropy back into them." Quote
taken from *1987 Current Biography Yearbook*, ed. Charles Moritz (New
York: The H. W. Wilson Company, 1987), p. 447.

In addition to his impressive scientific production, Prigogine co-
authored *Order out of Chaos* (New York: Bantam Books, 1984) with the
chemist, philosopher, and scientific historian Isabelle Stengers, a work
which expounds his theories for the layman.

39. *Éthique*, p. 120:
   La sexualité féminine s'harmoniserait peut-être mieux – s'il faut
   évoquer un modèle scientifique – avec ce que Prigogine appelle les structures "dissipatives", qui fonctionnnent par échange avec le monde
   extérieur, qui procèdent par paliers d'énergie et dont l'ordre ne revient pas
   à la recherche de l'équilibre mais au franchissement de seuils correspon-
   dant au dépassement du désordre ou de l'entropie sans décharge.
40. *Marine Lover*, p. 11.
41. *Nihilism*, p. 7.
42. *The Will to Power*, # 617, p. 330.
43. *Marine Lover*, p. 26.
44. Ibid., p. 60.
45. See Maurice Blanchot, "The Gaze of Orpheus" in *The Gaze of Orpheus*,
   trans. Lydia Davis, ed. P. Adams Sitney (Barrytown, New York: Station
   Hill Press, 1981). In this essay, Blanchot muses upon the poetic signifi-
   cance(s) of Orpheus' descent into Hades in an attempt to retrieve Eury-
   dice, an attempt which to him is emblematic of the power and powerless-
   ness of art (p. 99):
   Yet Orpheus' work does not consist in securing the approach of this
   "point" [Eurydice, as the limit of what art can attain] by descending into
   the depths. His *work* is to bring it back into the daylight and in the daylight give it form, figure and reality. Orpheus can do anything except look
   this "point" in the face, look at the center of the night in the night. He can
   descend to it, he can draw it to him – an even stronger power – and he can
   draw it upwards, but only by keeping his back turned to it. This turning
   away is the only way he can approach it: this is the meaning of the concealment revealed in the night. But in the impulse of his migration
   Orpheus forgets the work he has to accomplish, and he has to forget it,
   because the ultimate requirement of his impulse is not that there should be
   a work, but that someone should stand and face this "point" and grasp the
   essence where this essence appears, where it is essential and essentially
   appearance: in the heart of the night.
46. *Marine Lover*, p. 56.
47. Ibid., pp. 56–57.
48. Ibid., p. 61.
49. Martin Heidegger, *Introduction to Metaphysics*, trans. Ralph Manheim
   (New York: Anchor Books, 1961), p. 11.
50. This implies that modern French has appropriated this prior Roman
   interpretation of the Greek words, and that the original Greek meanings

are hidden from view from the modern speaker. This does not, however, indicate an ill will on the part of the speaker. All it says is that Irigaray, in her reading of the Greek word, understands it in terms of the Roman translation/appropriation that occurred in the 1st century A.D.

51. Martin Heidegger, *Identity and Difference*, trans. Joan Stambaugh (New York: Harper & Row, 1969), pp. 50–51.
52. Martin Heidegger, *Poetry, Language, Thought*, trans. Albert Hofstadter (New York: Harper & Row, 1971), p. 42.
53. *Marine Lover*, p. 58.
54. Ibid., p. 46.
55. See Book XII in *The Odyssey of Homer*, trans. Richmond Lattimore (New York: Harper & Row, 1965), pp. 186–187.
56. *Spurs*, p. 38.
57. For Derrida, the always-already-structure for a past passivity that is older than presence and essence and that can never be fully activated in the present. In its "absolute past", the always-already effaces itself and retreats, leaving behind a mark/trace or a "signature", which can be re-traced in the thing from which it withdraws. Since the always-already can never be present itself, it is not a trace of an already constituted present. As such, it can only be thought negatively, as a condition of "possibility of impossibility" of essence, which for Derrida gives rise to his notion of indeterminacy.
58. *Marine Lover*, p. 48.
59. Ibid., pp. 48–49.
60. Martin Heidegger, "Letter on Humanism", trans. Frank A. Capuzzi in collaboration with J. Glenn Gray in *Martin Heidegger: Basic Writings*, ed. David Farrell Krell (New York: Harper & Row, 1977), p. 193.
61. Martin Heidegger, *On Being and Time*, trans. Joan Stambaugh (New York: Harper & Row, 1972), p. 56.
62. Ibid., p. 71.
63. *Speculum*, p. 262.
64. Ibid., p. 263.
65. Luce Irigaray, *Speculum of the Other Woman*, pp. 262–263.
66. *On Time and Being*, p. 71.
67. *Identity and Difference*, p. 59.
68. Ibid., p. 60.
69. See *Le corps-à-corps avec la mère*, p. 43:
    Je voulais faire à l'origine une espèce de tétralogie qui aurait abordé le problème des quatres éléments: l'eau, l'air, le feu, la terre, appliquée à des philosophes plus proches de nous, et aussi mettre en cause la tradition philosophique, notamment du côté du féminin. Il faut interroger ce qui, dans une tradition présocratique, a été refoulé, censuré, oublié de l'élémentaire.
70. Martin Heidegger, "Logos" (Heraclitus, Fragment B 50) in *Early Greek Thinking*, trans. David Farrell Krell and Frank A. Capuzzi (London/New York: Harper & Row, 1975), pp. 59–78.
71. See Chapter I: "Theoretical Preliminaries."
72. *Being and Time*, p. 59.

73. *Early Greek Thinking*, p. 71.
74. *Marine Lover*, p. 64.
75. Ibid., p. 65.
76. Ibid., p. 67.
77. *Nihilism*, p. 214.
78. *Marine Lover*, p. 69.
79. Ibid., pp. 69–70.
80. *Éperons*, pp. 70–82.
81. See Margaret Whitford, *Luce Irigaray: Philosophy in the Feminine*.
82. *Marine Lover*, p. 70.
83. *Marine Lover*, p. 72.
84. Ibid., p. 72.
85. For an in-depth study of the inter-relationship between Lou Andreas-Salomé and Nietzsche, see Carolyn Arthur Martin, "The Death of 'God,' the Limits of 'Man,' and the Meanings of 'Woman:' The Work and the Legends of Lou Andreas-Salomé." Diss. University of Wisconsin-Madison, 1985.
86. *Marine Lover*, p. 71.
87. Ibid., p. 72.
88. *Marine Lover*, p. 71.
89. *Speculum*, p. 133.
90. See "The Blind Spot of an Old Dream of Symmetry" in *Speculum*, where Irigaray deconstructs Freud's essay on "Femininity" in *New Introductory Lectures on Psychoanalysis*, trans. James Strachey (New York: Standard Edition, Vol. XXII, 1933).
91. See Luce Irigaray, "Women's Exile", *Ideology and Consciousness*, Vol. 6, no. 1 (1977).
92. *Éthique*, p. 14:
   Il est vrai que, pour que l'oeuvre de la différence sexuelle ait lieu, il faut une revolution de pensée, et d'éthique. Tout est a réinterpreter dans les relations entre le sujet et le discours, le sujet est le monde, le sujet et le cosmique, le micro et le macrocosme.
93. See Naomi Schor's similar conclusion in "This Essentialism Which Is Not One", where she reads Irigaray's theoretical explorations of sexual difference as a transvaluation. (p. 21)
94. See my deliberation on the connection between Nietzsche and Descartes as viewed by Heidegger in Chapter II, pp. 23–32.
95. See for example Irigaray's reading of Lacan in "The 'Mechanics' of Fluids" in *This Sex Which Is Not One*, pp. 105–116.

Chapter IV

1. Friedrich Nietzsche, *Beyond Good and Evil: Prelude to a Philosophy of the Future*, trans. Walter Kaufmann (New York: Vintage Books, 1966).

2. See Heidegger's essay "The Raging Discordance between Truth and Art" in his first volume on Nietzsche, *The Will to Power as Art*, trans. David Ferrell Krell (New York: Harper & Row, 1979), pp. 142–150. In this essay he discusses the following statement from Nietzsche, which Nietzsche jotted down in 1888 during his preparation for *The Birth of Tragedy*, trans. Walter Kaufmann (New York: Vintage Books, 1967):

> Very early in my life I took the question of the relation of *art* to *truth* seriously: and even now I stand in holy dread in the face of this discordance. (XIV, 368)

3. *Beyond Good and Evil*, # 232, p. 163.

4. *Marine Lover*, p. 77.

5. Interestingly, because Irigaray reads Plato through Nietzsche, she accepts Nietzsche's understanding of what *eidos* means in Plato despite the fact that she diverges from him when it comes to the Nietzschean use of this appropriation of Plato. Heidegger, however, disagrees with Nietzsche in his essay "The Question Concerning Technology", in *The Question Concerning Technology and Other Essays* where he shows how the Platonic *eidos* has been reductively appropriated:

> We, late born, are no longer in a position to appreciate the significance of Plato's daring to use the word *eidos* for that which in everything and in each particular thing endures as present. For *eidos*, in the common speech, meant the outward aspect [Ansicht] that a visible thing offers to the physical eye. Plato exacts of this word, however, something utterly extraordinary: that it name what precisely is not and never will be perceivable with physical eyes. But even this is by no means the full extent of what is extraordinary here. For *idea* names not only the nonsensuous aspect of what is physically visible. Aspect (*idea*) names and is, also, *that which constitutes the essence of the audible, the tasteable, the tactile*, in everything that is in any way accessible. (p. 20)

What Heidegger brings to light in this quote might in fact upset both the Nietzschean appropriation of Plato and Irigaray's ensuing critique of Nietzsche. By creating "a raging discordance" between the supra-sensuous *eidos* as truth and the sensuous mater-ial as art, Nietzsche and the dominant metaphysical tradition before him have left out the *material* potential in the Platonic understanding of the *idea(l)*.

Nietzsche's work rests upon this radical separation between the two realms, and Irigaray's reading likewise rests on this fundamental assumption. The question would have to be posed, however, concerning what the possible implications of Heidegger's insight might bring to Irigaray's thinking on *le féminin*.

6. *Beyond Good and Evil*, # 232, pp. 162–163.

7. Ibid., p. 163.

8. Ibid., # 232, p. 164.

9. Aristophanes, *Lysistrata*, trans. Douglass Parker, ed. William Arrowsmith (New York: New American Library, 1964).

10. Ibid., p. 101.

11. The prime example of this tragic disintegration is found in the fate of

Oedipus, who is both blinded, robbed of his kingdom and exiled from the polis.

12. *Marine Lover*, p. 78.
13. Sigmund Freud, *Dora*: An Analysis of a Case of Hysteria, ed. Philip Rieff (New York: Collier Books, 1963), p. 22.
14. Friedrich Nietzsche, *The Birth of Tragedy*, trans. Walter Kaufmann (New York: Vintage Books, 1967).
15. Sophocles, *Oedipus the King* in *Greek Tragedies*: Volume 1, eds. David Greene and David Lattimore (Chicago: The University of Chicago Press, 1942).
16. *The Birth of Tragedy*, p. 69.
17. *Twilight of the Idols* in *The Portable Nietzsche*, p. 485.
18. This passage is included under the section "How the 'True World' finally became a Fable", whose first part is called "History of an Error." I refer to the passage in Chapter I when dealing with Derrida's reading of Heidegger and Nietzsche on the question of the "History of an Error" in *Éperons*.
19. *Spurs*, p. 97.
20. Friedrich Nietzsche, *The Gay Science*, trans. Walter Kaufmann (New York: Vintage Books, 1974), # 60, p. 124.
21. *Marine Lover*, p. 79.
22. *Twilight*, p. 485.
23. Ibid., p. 486.
24. *Marine Lover*, p. 79.
25. The question of castration (of woman) in the scenography of the *same* likewise constitute the focus in Irigaray's critique of the Freudian paradigm of sexual identity and psycho-sexual development in her essay "La tâche aveugle d'un vieux rêve de symétrie" in *Speculum*, pp. 9–162. In a deconstructive gesture, Irigaray sets out to unmask Freud's illusory positioning of himself as the philosopher-scientist-thinker who attempts to speak the "truth" of female sexuality. Even though Irigaray grants Freud the function as "underminer" of Western philosophical discourse of certitude through his introduction of the *unconscious* and its specific mechanisms, she nevertheless sees in his project a phallic positioning as lawmaker and truth-speaker, which must always rely on the solid ground of subjective consciousness and the reliability of the logos understood as reasonable language. The female body becomes then invaded by this masculine cartography – a morpho-logic of the masculine, isomorphic with the masculine sex which privileges unity, the stable form of the self, of the specularized visible, in short of the erection, which of course stands for the becoming of the form.

   In Freud's endeavor to construct a theory of (masculine) sexuality in which the penis gains a fetishized position of norm or "yardstick" against which female sexuality is compared or measured, woman's body and sexuality cannot function as other than "lack", "deficiency" or "non-presence." Her failure to exhibit only *one* organ becomes in phallocentric optics an evidence of her *not having any sex*, thus a castrated man. Through his appropriation of the female body, Freud is capable of erecting a theory of female sexuality which is based on a model that is fundamentally foreign to her and to the myoptic phallic vision renders *"un rien à voir"*. Woman thus comes to represent this "nothing to see" that gains the signification both of penis envy bestowed upon her as well as a "horrific" vision of the castrated man, which feeds his own "fear of castration".

26. Ibid., p. 80.
27. Ibid., p. 80.
28. Ibid., p. 87.
29. Ibid., p. 83.
30. Ibid., p. 83.
31. Ibid., p. 85.
32. See Luce Irigaray, "Women's Exile", *Ideology and Consciousness*, Vol. 1 (May 1977), pp. 57–76, an interview with Luce Irigaray which was first published under the title "Kvinner i eksil" in *Seks samtaler om psykiatri*, eds. S. Haugsgjerd and F. Engelstad (Oslo: Pax Forlag, 1978). Irigaray here states:

Anyway, one discovers here the question of the criteria of universality which dominate the whole Western thought, and thus psychoanalysis. When one defines the unconscious in terms of universal characteristics, one does not wonder whether these characteristics are valid for women also. I do not think that women, in fact, have an unconscious operating in the same way as that of men. Even the fact that women possess an unconscious is not self-evident. It is possible that one has been imposed on them. But to say that woman's sexuality is naturally subject to processes of repression, sublimation etc., that's very doubtful. I would rather frame the following question: *are women not, partly, the unconscious?* [My emphasis] That is, is there not in what has been historically constituted as the 'unconscious,' some censored, repressed element of the feminine? Certain functional criteria attributed to the unconscious, like non-contradiction, contiguity, etc., are, I think, close to female sexuality and language. (pp. 69–70)

33. *Marine Lover*, p. 86.
34. *Marine Lover*, p. 86.
35. Shoshana Felman has posed similar questions to Irigaray in her article entitled "The Critical Phallacy", *Diacritics* (Winter 1975). I quote:

If "the woman" is precisely the Other of any conceivable Western theoretical locus of speech, how can the woman as such be speaking in this book? Who is speaking here, and who is assessing the otherness of the woman? If, as Luce Irigaray suggests, the woman's silence or the repression of her capacity to speak, are constitutive of philosophy and of theoretical discourse as such, from what theoretical locus is Luce Irigaray herself speaking in order to develop her own theoretical discourse about women? Is she speaking *as* a woman, or *in the place of* the (silent) woman, *for* the woman, *in the name of* the woman? Is it enough to *be* a woman in order to *speak as* a woman? Is "speaking as a woman" a fact determined by some biological *condition* or by a strategic, theoretical *position*, by anatomy or by culture? What if "speaking as a woman" were not a simple "natural" fact, could not be taken for granted? (p 3).

36. *Marine Lover*, p. 90 (my translation):
    "Le hasard – la donne. Ne peut se donner que pour ce qu'il/elle n'est pas."
37. *Being and Time*, p. 63.
38. This is the title for the second part of Heidegger's *Nihilism* volume, pp. 197–252.
39. *Nihilism*, p. 228.
40. Ibid., p. 228.
41. Ibid., p. 229.
42. Ibid., p. 233.
43. *Marine Lover*, p. 89; *Amante marine*, p. 95.
44. Ibid., p. 89.
45. See Chapter III.
46. *Marine Lover*, p. 89.
47. See Heidegger's *Identity and Difference*.
48. See Immanuel Kant, *The Critique of Pure Reason*, trans. Norman Kemp Smith (New York: St. Martin's Press, 1965).
49. *Marine Lover*, p. 90.
50. Ibid., p. 91.
51. Ibid., p. 92.
52. *Identity and Difference*, pp. 50–51.
53. Ibid., p. 51.
54. *On Time and Being*, p. 3.
55. *The Gay Science*, p. 272.
56. Ibid., p. 271.
57. *Marine Lover*, p. 94.
58. Ibid., p. 94.
59. Ibid., p. 94.
60. *"Mythos"* is usually translated as "the telling word" which creates man in his world, that is, in his interrelationship with the cosmos, the gods and other beings.
61. Aeschylus, *Oresteia*, trans. Richmond Lattimore (Chicago: The University of Chicago Press, 1953).
62. Ibid., *The Eumenides*, p. 161, ll. 736–738.
63. Ibid., p. 158, ll. 658–666.
64. *Marine Lover*, p. 96.
65. *The Eumenides* in the *Oresteia*, p. 163, ll. 804–807.
66. Ibid., p. 171, ll. 1036–1039.
67. See Plato's *Apology*, trans. Moses Hadas (Chicago: Gateway Editions, 1953).
68. *Marine Love*, p. 98.
69. *L'oubli de l'air*, p. 81.
70. See Martin Heidegger's "The Question Concerning Technology" in *The Question Concerning Technology and Other Essays*, trans. William Lowitt (New York: Harper & Row, 1977), pp. 3–35. In this essay, Heidegger establishes a connection between the appropriations of *techne* in Western metaphysics and reveals how it has given rise to the predomi-

nantly technological enframing of science and philosophy.

71. *L'oubli de l'air*, p. 81.
72. See Chapter III on the question of the appropriation of *logos* in Roman language into "reason" and "adequation".
73. *Amante marine*, p. 109. It should be noted that truth in this context is not to be confounded with *aletheia* in the Pre-Socratic understanding of the word. Athena exemplifies truth in the sense of the repetition, *mimesis* or correspondence that speaks of truth's relationship to appearance.
74. *The Gay Science*, # 60, p. 123.
75. *Marine Lover*, pp. 104–105.
76. In *Spurs*, Derrida attempts to open up Nietzsche's text through the metaphors of the sail and of the umbrella, which in Derrida's view, both have the potential to contain a difference *within*, that is, they might signify both a phallic and a vaginal image due to their multiple forms containing both the (phallic) pointed object as well as the (vaginal) folds.
77. *The Gay Science*, # 59, p. 122.
78. Ibid., # 70, p. 127.
79. In the following passage from *Beyond Good and Evil*, Dionysus, in the voice of the philosopher, likens Ariadne to a man by making the following remarks:
    Thus he once said: "Under certain circumstances I love what is human" – and with this he alluded to Ariadne who was present – "man is to my mind an agreeable, courageous, inventive animal that has no equal on earth; it finds its way in the labyrinth. I am well disposed towards him: I often reflect how I might yet advance him and make him stronger, more evil, and more profound than he is." (# 295, p. 236)
80. *Marine Lover*, p. 111.
81. Ibid., p. 113.
82. Ibid., p. 114.
83. See *The Odyssey of Homer*, Ovid's *Metamorphoses*, Virgil's *Aeneid* and Dante's *Inferno*, where the respective poets guide their characters to the underworld in order to provide them with a privileged (poetic) access into that which "cannot be seen", but which nevertheless shapes the destiny of each and every one of them, namely mortality, the ultimate signifier of temporality.
84. See *Being and Time*, Part 1, Section II.
85. Ibid., pp. 115–116.
86. *L'oubli de l'air*, p. 130:
    L'être ne trouve-t-il son fondement dans une immédiateté sensible encore imparlée? Dans un silence sur ce qui alimente secrètement la pensée? L'indit ou l'indicible d'un rapport de l'homme à une nature échappant a son *logos*. Se donnant au lieu innommé du rassemblement de l'apport des organes de tous ses sens. Reçu qu'il reprojette en un monde et ses choses. Recréant ainsi le tout, et faisant de chacune toutes, et de toutes chacune, sans que le secret de cette production lui apparaisse jamais.

Conclusion

1. It is possible to object to Irigaray's somewhat selective reading of Zarathoustra in regard to his "flight" by emphasizing that he embodies both realms, that is, the "transcendental" (through the figure of the eagle) as well as the "material" (through the figure of the serpent). Furthermore, it is interesting to note that all of Nietzsche's *irony* in his projection of Zarathoustra seems to be completely lost in Irigaray's reading.

2. What seems to be lost in Irigaray's interpretation of Zarathoustra's pronouncement, is that Nietzsche uses the figure of "woman" to think the question of time rather than speaking of the social class of women.

3. This is perhaps the way in which Irigaray falls back into a Lacanian phenomenology of "presence" and "absence" as put forth in his "Dasein psychoanalysis" of his earlier production.

4. One could, however, posit that Zeus, as opposed to Athena and Apollo, represents the "law of the Mother" in his accepting to kill Cronos as requested by Rhea. However, in the Attic tragedy, the gods are being defined more and more in terms of their relationship to the *polis*, thereby gradually becoming inscribed into the "Law of the Father".

5. See Chapter 4, note # 5, pp. 236–237, where I include a reference to Heidegger's reading of Plato on the question of *eidos*.

6. *The Question Concerning Technology*, p. 20.

Select Bibliography

Aeschylus. *Oresteia*. Trans. Richmond Lattimore. Chigago: The University of Chicago Press, 1953.

Aristophanes. *Lysistrata*. Trans. Douglass Parker. Ed. William Arrowsmith. New York: New American Library, 1964.

Baudrillard, Jean. *Simulations*. Trans. Paul Foss et al. New York: Semiotext(e) Inc., 1983.

Beckwith, Sarah. "A Very Material Mysticism: The Medieval Mysticism of Margaret Kempe." In *Medieval Literature: Criticism, Ideology, and History*. Ed. David Aers. New York: St. Martin's Press, 1986, 34–57.

Berg, Elizabeth L. "The Third Woman." *Diacritics* 12, 2 (1982), 11–20.

Blanchot, Maurice. *The Gaze of Orpheus*. Trans. Lydia Davis. Ed. P. Adams Sitney. Barrytown, New York: Station Hill Press, 1981.

Burke, Carolyn. "Irigaray through the Looking Glass." *Feminist Studies* 7, 2 (Summer 1981), 288–306.

Cixous, Hélène. "The Laugh of the Medusa". Trans. Keith and Paula Cohen. In *New French Feminisms*. Eds. I. de Courtivron & E. Marks. New York: Shocken Books, 1981, pp.245–265.

____ and Clément, Catherine. *La jeune née*. Paris: 10/18, 1977.

Dante Alighieri. *Inferno*. In *The Divine Comedy*. Trans. John D. Sinclair. New York: Oxford University Press, 1939.

Derrida, Jacques. *Dissemination*. Trans. Barbara Johnson. Chicago: The University of Chicago Press, 1978.

_____. *Positions*. Trans. Alan Bass. Chicago: The University of Chicago Press, 1981.

_____. *Margins of Philosophy*. Trans. Alan Bass. Chicago: The University of Chicago Press, 1982.

Felman, Shoshana. "The Critical Phallacy." *Diacritics*. (Winter 1975), 2–10.

_____. *La folie et la chose littéraire*. Paris: Les Éditions de Seuil, 1978.

Féral, Josette. "Antigone or the Irony of the Tribe." Trans. Alice Jardine and Tom Gora. *Diacritics* 7/8 (Fall 1978), 2–14.

Foucault, Michel. *The History of Sexuality*. Vol. I. Trans. Robert Hurley. New York: Random House, 1980.

Freeman, Barbara. "Irigaray at *The Symposium*: Speaking Otherwise." *Oxford Literary Review* 8, 1–2: *Sexual Difference* (1986), 170–177.

Freud, Sigmund. *Beyond the Pleasure Principle*. Trans. James Strachey. New

York: Norton, 1959.

_____. *Dora: An Analysis of a Case of Hysteria*. Ed. Philip Rieff. New York: Collier Books, 1963.

_____. *The Interpretation of Dreams*. Trans and ed. James Strachey. New York: Avon Books, 1965.

Gallop, Jane. *The Daughter's Seduction: Feminism and Psychoanalysis*. Ithaca: Cornell University Press, 1982.

_____. "Quand nos lèvres s'écrivent: Irigaray's Body Politic." *Romanic Review* 74, 1 (1983), 77–83.

Elizabeth Gross, "Irigaray and the Divine." *Local Consumption Papers*, no. 9 (1986).

_____. "Irigaray and Sexual Difference." *Australian Feminist Studies* 2 (Autumn 1986) 63–77.

_____. "Derrida, Irigaray and Deconstruction." In "Leftwright", *Intervention* 20 (1986); 70–81.

_____. "Philosophy, Subjectivity and the Body: Kristeva and Irigaray." In E. Grosz and C. Pateman, eds, *Feminist Challenges: Social and Political Theory*. Sydney: Allen & Unwin, 1986, pp. 125–43.

Elizabeth Grosz. "Desire, the Body and Recent French Feminisms." *Intervention* 21–22 (1988); 28–33.

_____. "Notes towards a Corporal Feminism." *Australian Feminist Studies* 5 (Summer 1987), 1–16.

_____. *Sexual Subversions: Three French Feminists*. Sydney: Allen & Unwin, 1989.

Heidegger, Martin. *Being and Time*. Trans. John Macquarrie and Edward Robinson. New York: Harper & Row, 1962.

_____. *Early Greek Thinking*. Trans. David Farrell Krell and Frank A. Capuzzi. New York: Harper & Row, 1975.

_____. and Fink, Eugene. *Heraklitus Seminar: 1966/67*. Trans. Charles H. Seibert. Alabama: University of Alabama Press, 1982.

_____. *Identity and Difference*. Trans. Joan Stambaugh. New York: Harper & Row, 1969.

_____. *Introduction to Metaphysics*. Trans. Ralph Mannheim. New York: Anchor Books, 1961.

_____. "Letter on Humanism." *Martin Heidegger: Basic Writings*. Trans. Frank A. Capuzzi. Ed. David Farrell Krell. New York: Harper & Row, 1977.

_____. *Nietzsche*, Vol. I: *The Will to Power as Art*. Trans. David Farrell Krell. New York: Harper & Row, 1979.

_____. *Nietzsche*, Vol. IV: *Nihilism*. Trans. David Farrell Krell. New York: Harper & Row, 1982.

_____. *On Time and Being*. Trans. Joan Staumbach. New York: Harper & Row, 1969.

_____. *On the Way to Language*. Trans. Peter D. Hertz. New York: Harper & Row, 1971.

_____. *Poetry, Language, Thought*. Trans. Albert Hofstadter. New York: Harper & Row, 1971.

_____. *The Question Concerning Technology and Other Essays*. Trans. William Lowitt. New York: Harper & Row, 1977.

Hirsh, Elizabeth A. "New Eyes: H.D., Modernism, and the Psychoanalysis of Seeing." *Literature and Psychology* 32, 3 (1986), 1–10.

Homer. *The Odyssey of Homer*. Trans. Richmond Lattimore. New York: Harper & Row, 1965.

Irigaray, Luce. *Amante marine de Friedrich Nietzsche*. Paris: Les Éditions de Minuit, 1980.

_____. *Le corps-à-corps avec la mère*. Montréal: les Éditions de la pleine lune, 1981.

_____. *La croyance même*. Paris: Éditions Galilée, 1983.

_____. *Et l'une ne bouge pas sans l'autre*. Paris: Les Éditions de Minuit, 1979.

_____. *Éthique de la différence sexuelle*. Paris: Les Éditions de Minuit, 1984.

_____. "Is the Subject of Science Sexed?" Trans. Edith Oberle. *Cultural Critique* 1 (Fall 1985), 73–88.

_____. *Le langage des déments*. Paris: Éditions Mouton, 1973.

_____. *Marine Lover of Friedrich Nietzsche*. Trans. Gillian C. Gill. New York: Columbia University Press, 1991.

_____. *L'oubli de l'air. Chez Martin Heidegger*. Paris: Les Éditions de Minuit, 1983.

_____. *Parler n'est jamais neutre*. Paris: Les Éditions de Minuit, 1985.

_____. *Passions élémentaires*. Paris: Les Éditions de Minuit, 1982.

_____. *Ce sexe qui n'en est pas un*. Paris: Les Éditions de Minuit, 1977.

_____. *Sexes et parentés*. Paris: Les Éditions de Minuit, 1987.

_____. *Speculum de l'autre femme*. Paris: Les Éditions de Minuit, 1974.

_____. *Speculum of the Other Woman*. Trans. Gillian C. Gill. Ithaca: Cornell University Press, 1985.

_____. *This Sex Which Is Not One*. Trans. Catherine Porter. Ithaca: Cornell University Press, 1985.

_____. "Women's Exile." *Ideology and Consciousness*, 6, 1 (1977), 57–77.

Jardine, Alice. *Gynesis: Configurations of Woman and Modernity*. Ithaca: Cornell University Press, 1985.

Jones, Ann Rosalind. "Writing the Body: Toward an Understanding of L'Écriture féminine." *Feminist Studies* 7, 2 (Summer 1981), 247–263.

Kant, Immanuel. *The Critique of Pure Reason*. Trans. Norman Kemp Smith. New York: St. Martin Press, 1929.

Kristeva, Julia. *La Révolution du langage poétique*. Paris, Les Éditions du Seuil, 1974.

Lacan, Jacques. *Écrits I*. Paris: Les Éditions de Seuil, 1970.

_____. *Écrits II*. Paris: Les Éditions de Seuil, 1971.

_____. *Feminine Sexuality: Jacques Lacan and the école freudienne*. Trans. and Ed. Jacqueline Rose and Juliet Mitchell. New York: Norton, 1982.

_____. *The Language of the Self: The Function of Language in Psychoanalysis*. Trans. Anthony Wilden. New York: Delta Books, 1968.

_____. "Traduction de 'logos' de Heidegger." *La Psychanalyse* 1 (1956), 56–79.

Marks, Elaine and Courtivron, Isabelle. *New French Feminisms: An Anthology*. New York: Shocken Books, 1981.

Martin, Carolyn Arthur. "The Death of 'God,' the Limits of 'Man,' and the Meanings of 'Woman:' The Work and the Legends of Lou Andreas-Salomé." Diss. University of Wisconsin-Madison, 1985.

Moi, Toril, Ed. *The Kristeva Reader*. Oxford: Basil Blackwell, 1986.

_____. *Sexual/Textual Politics*. New York: Methuen, 1985.

Moritz, Charles, ed. *1987 Current Biography Yearbook*. New York: The H.W. Wilson Company, 1987.

Neuman, Shirley. "Importing Difference." *In Amazing Space: Canadian Women Writing*. Eds. Shirley Neuman and Smaro Kamboureli. Edmonton: Longspoon Press, 1986, 392–405.

Nietzsche, Friedrich. *Beyond Good and Evil: Prelude to a Philosophy of the Future*. Trans. Walter Kaufmann. New York: Vintage Books, 1966.

_____. *The Birth of Tragedy and The Case of Wagner*. Trans. Walter Kaufmann. New York: Vintage Books, 1967.

_____. *The Gay Science*. Trans. Walter Kaufmann. New York: Vintage Books, 1974.

_____. *Thus Spoke Zarathoustra*. In *The Portable Nietzsche*. Trans. and Ed. Walter Kaufmann. New York: The Viking Press, 1968, 103–439.

_____. *The Twilight of the Idols*. In *The Portable Nietzsche*. Trans. and Ed. Walter Kaufmann. New York: The Viking Press, 1968, 463–563.

_____. *The Will to Power*. Trans. and Ed. Walter Kaufmann. New York: Vintage Books, 1967.

Ovid. *The Metamorphoses*. Trans. Rolfe Humphries. Bloomington: Indiana University Press, 1955.

Parker, Patricia. *Literary Fat Ladies: Rhetoric, Gender, Property*. London: Methuen, 1987.

Plato. *Euthyphro, Crito, Apology, Symposium*. Trans. B. Jowett. Chicago: Gateway Editions, 1953.

_____. *Republic*. In *Dialogues of Plato*, Vol. II. Trans. B. Jowett. Oxford: The Clarendon Press, 1953,1–499.

Prigogine, Ilya and Stengers, Isabelle. *Order out of Chaos*. New York: Bantam Books, 1984.

Ricoeur, Paul. *Freud and Philosophy: An Essay on Interpretation*. Trans. Denis Savage. New Haven: Yale University Press, 1970.

Riley, Denise. "Does Sex Have a History?" *New Formations* (Spring 1987).

Schor, Naomi. "This Essentialism Which Is Not One." Differences (2); 1–33–58.

Sedgewick, Eve Kosofsky. *Between Men: English Literature and Male Homosexual Desire*. New York: Columbia University Press, 1985.

Sophoeles. *Oedipus the King*. In *Greek Tragedies: Volume I*. Eds. David Greene and David Lattimore. Chicago: The University of Chicago Press, 1942.

Stanton, Domna. "Difference on Trial: A Critique of the Maternal Metaphor in Cixous, Irigaray, and Kristeva." In *The Poetics of Gender*. Ed. Nancy K. Miller. New York: Columbia University Press, 1986, 157–182.

Turkle, Sherry. *Psychoanalytic Politics: Freud's French Revolution.* New York: Basic Books, 1978.

Virgil. *The Aeneid of Virgil.* Trans. Allen Mandelbaum. New York: Bantam Books, 1971.

Wenzel, Helene Vivienne. "Introduction to Luce Irigaray's 'And the One Doesn't Stir without the Other.'" *Signs: Journal of Women in Culture and Society* 7, 1 (Autumn 1981), 56–59.

Whitford, Margaret, Ed. *The Irigaray Reader.* Oxford: Basil Blackwell, 1991.

_____. "Luce Irigaray and the Female Imaginary: Speaking as a Woman." *Radical Philosophy* 21: 18–28.

_____. *Luce Irigaray: Philosophy in the Feminine.* London: Routledge, 1991.